LEADING FROM WITHIN

Developing Personal Direction

The Professional Practices in Adult Education and Human Resource Development Series explores issues and concerns of practitioners who work in the broad range of settings in adult and continuing education and human resource development.

The books are intended to provide information and strategies on how to make practice more effective for professionals and those they serve. They are written from a practical viewpoint and provide a forum for instructors, administrators, policy makers, counselors, trainers, managers, program and organizational developers, instructional designers, and other related professionals.

Editorial correspondence should be sent to the Editor-in-Chief:

Michael W. Galbraith
Florida Atlantic University
Department of Educational Leadership
College of Education
Boca Raton, FL 33431

LEADING FROM WITHIN

Developing Personal Direction

Nancy S. Huber

KRIEGER PUBLISHING COMPANY
MALABAR, FLORIDA
1998

Original Edition 1998

Printed and Published by
KRIEGER PUBLISHING COMPANY
KRIEGER DRIVE
MALABAR, FLORIDA 32950

Library of Congress Cataloging-In-Publication Data

Huber, Nancy S.
    Leading from within : developing personal direction / Nancy S.
Huber. — Original ed.
        p.   cm. — (The professional practices in adult education and
human resource development series)
    Includes bibliographical references (p.) and index.
    ISBN 1-57524-022-X (alk. paper)
    1. Leadership.   2. Leadership—Study and teaching.   I. Title.
II. Series.
HM141.H77   1998
303.3′4—dc21   98-13961
                                                                    CIP

10 9 8 7 6 5 4 3 2

CONTENTS

PREFACE

After more than a decade involved with communities and organizations in leadership education and organizational development, I was asked to design a leadership course and teach it in a college classroom setting. I quickly came to realize that things were quite different in the classroom. In my work with community groups, for example, participants knew why they wanted to learn to lead and they knew a great deal about the situation in which they would be operating. Although curious, students really didn't come to the course with a specific purpose for leading and had no contextual basis for their learning.

It soon became apparent that learning to lead demands that purposeful, contextual grounding. Until students knew why they wanted to lead, it was simply an exercise in learning ABOUT leadership rather than learning to DO leadership. At the same time, I discovered that the books I was perusing for possible use with my students were not what I needed to help bridge that gap. Some were contextually biased toward business and the corporate sector, some were limited to a particular field, some were intent on promotion of a particular model for leadership, and most of them continued to foster learning about leadership rather than engaging people in actually learning and leading at the same time.

I can remember as a teenager sitting in a second-year Latin class and hearing the teacher say on many occasions, "When I write MY Latin book . . . " After trying to find just the right book to use in my own leadership classes and workshops, I began to realize what she meant. This is not to say I am a self-proclaimed leadership expert. However, I have a sense of the interdependence of learning and leading born of my own experience. I wanted a book for those who want to lead, not simply to read about leadership.

Leading from Within: Developing Personal Direction is based on the assumption that we are all called to lead. Sometimes, coping with things the way they are is just not good enough. When we care enough to want to make a difference, we are ready to lead. This assumption is supported by my belief that leadership and title or position are only marginally related. You can lead wherever you are! Additionally, I believe that life-long learning and leadership are inextricably entwined. Learning while you lead involves examination of the context within which you intend to bring about change, and discovery of the leadership skills and concepts you will need to hone to be effective in that context.

Leading from Within was first conceived for use in the classroom. However, as it evolved, its purpose expanded. Written in a way that can serve the needs of individuals who have an interest in learning about leading, or who work within organizations and communities and wish to strengthen shared leadership, it is a book that can be very personal. It is neither an erudite study of the research and literature about leadership, nor a cookbook with page after page of tips, quotes, and recipes for success for those looking for a guaranteed trip to the top of the ladder complete with position and title. The purpose of *Leading from Within* goes beyond satisfying the needs of people who simply want to know about others who lead. It is for people who want to engage the process of leadership, either because of their passion for a preferred future where they live and work, or their involvement in a situation they feel compelled to change for the better. This book is about BEING a leader, DOING leadership. This book is about YOU!

Telling stories is one of the oldest and most effective ways to share learning. Thus, each chapter begins with a personal story or reflection designed to give meaning to the discussion that follows. We also learn by doing—through reflection, application, and reading. Therefore, at the end of each chapter, you will find suggestions to guide you through those processes.

Questions for reflection and journaling are intended to provoke deeper exploration of your personal thoughts and feelings while you are developing your capacity to lead. Learning activities are included to provide a way for you to apply the concepts or practice the skills presented in each chapter. Suggested readings and resources are listed at the end of each chapter, rather than as an annotated bibliography. The intent is to facilitate additional investigation of those topics that are of particular interest to you and to help you personalize your learning. These readings and resources are included with the references at the end of the book.

The chapters are presented in a sequence that has proven useful. However, you are encouraged to begin anywhere that makes sense to you. Chapter 1 lays out some basic tools to use throughout the book—a simple framework for exploring leadership and some guidelines for journaling. In Chapter 2, the literature serves as the basis for beginning to explore the meaning of leadership.

Beginning with Chapter 3, the reader is asked to personalize the learning experience by bringing his or her own reason for leading into focus. Chapter 4 continues the process by encouraging a thorough examination of the context within which the leader intends to bring about change. In Chapter 5, the process for uncovering a personal philosophy of leadership is engaged and the reader is asked to develop a credo statement.

Since leadership doesn't happen in a vacuum, Chapter 6 shifts the focus to consideration of others involved in the leadership relationship. This idea is expanded in Chapter 7 which explores the meaning of community.

Chapter 8 discusses the interdependent relationship between lifelong learning and leading and includes a tool for designing a personal leadership development program. The final chapter touches on personal choices that you will make when you are being a leader, doing leadership. The focus is on leading with integrity which means being passionate, authentic, credible, and ethical.

Although some authors in the field might seem prepared to declare, "I have the answers to all your questions about leadership!" others might say, "I wish I could give you all the answers." Not me! I've always thought that good questions were more important than answers. It is really up to you. I can't tell you everything **YOU** need to know to be an effective leader. I won't tell you everything **I** know about learning and leading. None of us ever knows it all, but we can know enough. I wish you a journey through learning and leading filled with meaning and joy!

ACKNOWLEDGMENTS

Writing a book is not a solitary experience. There have been many people whose contributions have given life to *Leading from Within: Developing Personal Direction*. Those from whom I have learned about leading have my everlasting thanks. The list includes people with whom I have worked over the last decade or more, as either teacher or student, facilitator or learner. In particular, Jerry Apps has been mentor and friend, the catalyst when I began the journey into learning and leading. More recently, students in AED 401/501 (Leadership Concepts and Contexts) have been a source of insight and support. Two cohorts at The University of Arizona have read *Leading from Within* in its early stages to offer advice and encouragement. Thank you Sue Leverenz and Chris Johnson. A special thank you to several wonderful students who worked with me to research, record, and organize the best from a wealth of current leadership literature: Marie Louka, Mary Kate Czuppa, Valerie DeSanta, and Inga Beck.

I'd also like to thank several professional cohorts whose contribution to *Leading from Within* is greatly appreciated. Several are mentioned in the text: David Sanderson, Michael Brazzel, and I served on a national committee together a number of years ago and it is from their work that I have adapted my approach to vision and mission development. In addition, Janet Ayers's continuum for leadership development was modified to become the leadership education matrix presented in Chapter 8. Daryl Heasley and Deborah Preston spent a semester of their sabbatical year here in Arizona. It was an association that coincided with some of my early attempts to sort out and write down what this book was about. I appreciate their interest in my work and their enduring friendship.

   Leading from Within would not have come to fruition without the love and support of family and friends. Thanks to Karen for pushing, prodding, and believing in me. Thanks to Laurie for linguistic assistance delivered with great kindness. Thanks to Carrie for lovingly putting together the pieces and formatting the early drafts. Thanks to Ben and Nancy for artistic advice and unfailing support. Thanks to Mary for her story and for her massages when energy gave out and muscles ached. Thanks to Sharon, Tom, Pete, and Anita for cheering me on. And last, thanks to Roger—my champion and soulmate—for his love and support.

THE AUTHOR

Nancy S. Huber is a leadership educator who may be found working with "students" in the classroom at The University of Arizona, in board rooms, at conferences, in community meeting places, and in the most casual of settings. She teaches from the heart, modeling what she espouses within her personal working philosophy of leadership. She draws upon an extensive library of contemporary writers and infuses her teaching with real life experiences.

The author brings a variety of experience to her work. As a graduate student in her mid-thirties, she formed some opinions about lifelong learning which shape her current teaching. She holds both an M.S. and a Ph.D. from the University of Wisconsin where she explored adult education and leadership in the Department of Continuing and Vocational Education. Since 1985, she has been at The University of Arizona where she has held a number of positions. For five years, she gave leadership to the Community Leadership and Resource Development program for Cooperative Extension in Arizona. While an extension employee, she designed and implemented Leadership for Transformation, a western region leadership development program. She went on to work for the College of Education as an educational outreach specialist. In 1996, she completed a two-year association with the Continuous Organizational Renewal (CORe) program at The University of Arizona, serving as the CORe Partner for Leadership and Outreach. During that time, she managed the President's Quality Leadership Program which focused on enhancing transformational leadership capacity among academic department heads.

Currently, as an associate professor in the College of Agriculture at The University of Arizona, the author teaches courses in both leadership and nonformal education while exploring the possibility of creating a program which would integrate lifelong learning and leadership across the disciplines. As both an adult educator and a strong advocate of the land-grant system's role in educational outreach, she continues to be available to work with organizations and individuals interested in leadership development.

CHAPTER 1

A Personal Look at Leadership

It was late in life before I called myself a leader. It was, in fact, during my second year as a returning adult student in graduate school at the University of Wisconsin. I had left Maine on the heels of a divorce and bankruptcy to embark on the second half of my life. After volunteering for several years in the dual capacity of advisor and advocate for the Cooperative Extension Service, my involvement led to work at a national level where I came to know most of the extension directors and agriculture deans in the land grant system. When my life as traditional homemaker and part-time manager of a small family business came to a close, they had encouraged me to pursue the necessary academic degrees to legitimize myself as a paid employee within the organization I had served for many years.

One of the projects I undertook as a graduate assistant was in support of the design and implementation of the emerging Wisconsin Rural Leadership Program. As a presenter at the introductory session with the first group of participants, I prepared my notes on what I thought it meant to take responsibility for leadership. It was then that I first recognized myself as a leader. Why did this not occur to me until that moment? The answer, I believe, lies in historical notions about power, position and leadership skills, and the leadership models they spawned. This frame of reference for my early understanding of leadership emphasized hierarchy and credentials.

Saying out loud that I was a leader marked an awakening of my sense of self as one who practiced leadership. Previously, I might not have been readily perceived as a leader at all. Insofar as leadership and power are couched in terms of position and wealth, I had neither. I was a volunteer serving an organization that I believed in and had been associated with since I was a teenager. In the old framework, I should have been unsure of my leadership skills because I had little formal training. But, intuitively I knew I was a leader and that the capacity to lead was growing within me. "Volunteer" is but one of many ways to say "leader."

One of the most stark insights came to me when I was considering my financial plight as a returning adult student. I wondered how I could be a highly regarded woman jetting across the country to attend meetings and testify at congressional hearings AND, at the same time, be a single mother buying clothes for my two teenagers at a secondhand thrift shop and pinching pennies every time I went to the grocery store. I felt as though half of me was living a lie—but which half? Because I knew I wasn't two people, I drew a mental line connecting the disparate points that defined me and recognized that somewhere on that continuum was the core of me, the sine qua non which was the essence of who I was fully engaged in becoming.

IN SEARCH OF A UNIVERSAL MODEL

The story above serves to illustrate that our understanding of leadership and of ourselves as leaders is often shaped by what others have taught us rather than by our own experience leading. Although there is merit in reflecting upon what writers and researchers have had to say ABOUT leadership, the discussion in this chapter will be cursory. We will look at a range of leadership models as preparation for creating a personalized framework for learning and leading before we move to the essence of this book, the DOING of leadership.

It sometimes seems that more has been written and yet less is understood about leadership than most topics in the current literature. It is no wonder that those who teach and write on the subject look for a model to explain their perspective of leadership. We are not without models to use as examples. Quite the opposite! Leadership models and theories abound in the literature. Some writers advocate a particular model which they have developed while others present a comprehensive and scholarly review of the development of leadership theory over time. In his overview of leadership studies, Rost (1991) provides an excellent synopsis of movements, myths, theories and rituals associated with trying to acquire an understanding of leadership. Similarly, Bass (1990) chronicles the development of leadership theory in the last two centuries.

The early great-man theories derived from a rationalist perspective which held that history is shaped by heroes, those who have inherited the right genes and who have the luck to be in the right place at the right time. This way of thinking led to the notion that certain traits differentiated leaders from the masses. Personality traits and character attributes were studied (and still are) to determine which qualities were essential for effective leadership to occur. When questions were raised concerning the influence of circumstance on the ability of the leader to function well, situational leadership theories were introduced. This point of view adhered to the principle that leaders emerge as a result of the condition of the times. Researchers' dissatisfaction with the comprehensiveness of the great-man theory, trait theory, or situational theory, has spawned numerous conceptual frameworks for studying and explaining the leadership phenomenon. Figure 1.1 recaps those described in Bass's (1990) comprehensive introduction to theories and models of leadership. Since my intent in writing this book is to provide a tool for leading rather than a compendium of the literature about leadership, I will refer you to either Bass or Rost for more in depth discussion if you wish to pursue an interest in leadership research and theory.

In the last decade, the popular press has exploded with variations and nuances of leadership theory. Both descriptive and prescriptive leadership books have been marketed heavily, written primarily with the corporate sector in mind. Metaphors and lists of key concepts have eased into the arena of models and theories as a way of describing the leadership phenomenon. For example, one can explore the metaphorical imagery inherent in *Managing As a Performing Art* (Vaill, 1989), *The Servant As Leader* (Greenleaf, 1991) and *A Peacock in the Land of Penguins*

Personal and Situational Theories:
>   great-man theories
>   trait theories
>   situational theories
>   personal-situational theories
>   psychoanalytic theories
>   political theories
>   humanistic theories
> Interaction and Social Learning Theories:
>   leader-role theory
>   theories of attainment of leadership role
>   reinforced-change theory
>   path-goal theory
>   contingency theory
> Theories and Models of Interactive Processes:
>   multiple-linkage model
>   multiple-screen model
>   vertical-dyad linkage
>   exchange theories
>   behavioral theories
>   communication theories
> Perceptual and Cognitive Theories:
>   attribution theories
>   information processing
>   open-systems analysis
>   rational deductive approach
> Hybrid Explanations:
>   transformational leadership

Figure 1.1 Theories and models (*Bass, 1990, Ch. 3*)

(Hateley & Schmidt, 1995). Similarly, the reader would expect prescriptive lists and pragmatic suggestions in *Ten Steps to a Learning Organization* (Kline & Saunders, 1993) and *The 7 Habits of Highly Effective People* (Covey, 1989).

All of these models and metaphors help us understand more about leadership. History informs the study of leadership, but it is not the same as being a leader, doing leadership. However, because *Leading from Within* is concerned with doing rather than simply knowing about leadership, I suggest a frame for learning and leading which allows both flexibility and direction. It is the simplest model I know—and the most personal. In fact, I hesitate to label it a model because it doesn't encompass a theoretical framework so much as it is simply a way of engaging in the act of leading. Ultimately, it comes down to applying leadership concepts and skills to the process of involving other people in changing things for the better. It embodies our natural response to instances where we recognize that simply coping with a situation is no longer appropriate.

There is a dilemma associated with trying to devise a universal model for leadership. Leading is a human process which involves complex relationships and interactions driven by convictions born of values. At the same time, leading is a simple reaction to a perceived need to make a difference—a response to a personal sense of inequity or a vision for a better way. We are all called to lead! Once I set pen to paper and try to depict what that looks like, I run the risk of excluding certain people or actions or settings. This is only natural because my perspective of leadership is deeply embedded in my values and beliefs and colored by my experience. Most people who attempt to design the universal leadership model do so because of their interest in research. They tend to believe that leadership is predictable and quantifiable. So, the dilemma arises from the need to understand leadership from a research perspective and the desire to know leadership from a personal point of view. In *Leading from Within*, my hope is that I can provide a means by which leading can be more easily engaged—a model which can be personalized in such a way that it guides our development as we learn and lead.

A WORKING MODEL FOR LEADING

The model I suggest is an attempt to create a tool for your learning and leading, a means for understanding and practicing leadership born of one person's experience finding and nurturing the leader within. It involves understanding some basic leadership concepts, discovering a personal reason for leading, and building partnerships within a community of interest with whom to bring about positive change. The framework is a simple one.

Consider a short phrase with two blanks to be filled in: LEADERSHIP FOR _____ WITH _____. In this phrase, the use of the term "leadership" denotes the process of defining the term and examining the underlying concepts and strategies. Initially, our exploration of the concepts will be minimal, intended to simply lay some groundwork. Then we will return to examine concepts and skills once we know just what it is we need to know within our leadership context.

The first blank should be filled in with your passion, your reason for leading. It is this purpose that provides the basis for determining which leadership concepts and skills you will ultimately need to learn and apply. Your purpose may be refined as you probe the context of your issue and home in on just what motivates you to engage in learning leadership. The second blank is for those who are part of the situation in which you want to bring about change, stakeholders who are affected by it, or who might influence it. Because leadership is not a singular activity, you will want to look for collaborators among others who have a stake in the outcome of whatever change occurs. You could find this is really a long list rather than a word or two that fills the blank.

In the very simplest of terms, the completed phrase might read: LEADERSHIP FOR change WITH stakeholders . In theory, filling in the blanks and then coming to understand and apply leadership concepts and skills implied by this activity is the design for your learning and leading. It is a frame of reference that has grown out of my own experiences leading, has allowed me to build on my strengths, and has replaced my early insecurities about not having a title or credentials.

The simplicity of this approach assumes that leading and lifelong learning go hand in hand. This link is echoed in some of the recent leadership literature: *Learning As a Way of Being* (Vaill, 1996), *Leadership and the New Science* (Wheatley, 1992) and *Sculpting the Learning Organization* (Watkins & Marsick,

1993). Our education certainly doesn't stop dramatically just as soon as we receive that final diploma and say goodbye to the formal classroom. Good leaders are lifelong learners. Similarly, most who are committed to lifelong learning are developing their capacity to lead. This concept will be expanded in Chapter 8.

The fact that I teach courses in both leadership and lifelong learning seems both logical and synergistic to me. I prefer learning situations that are interactive. Frankly, I can't imagine lecturing someone to lead! As a way of enriching the dialogue, I frequently ask students or workshop participants, "What does this mean to you? How can you take what we discuss and find meaning in it for you, personally?" As you delve into subsequent chapters, stop now and then to ask yourself what it means to you.

REFLECTION AND JOURNALING

Reflecting on the meaning of leadership stories and concepts as we read and discuss is the key to deeper learning. Contemplative thinking, even meditation, is the mind's way of making sense of information and relating new ideas to our existing base of knowledge.

I believe journaling is an important way to record reflections while tracking personal growth and development in the study and practice of leadership. When I say this in my classes, I can almost hear some students say to themselves, "Oh, great! That means I'll have to spend time at the end of the semester writing up a journal to pass in for a grade. I hope it doesn't have to be too long." Then I tell them that I think journaling is important enough to take at least ten minutes just before the close of each class session to write in their journals. Some eyebrows go up. Furthermore, as I hand out spiral bound notebooks, I explain that I will even provide a journal so they won't have to purchase one. As you delve into *Leading from Within*, keep a journal close by and make good use of it. Here are some general guidelines to get you started:

- If you are new to journaling, don't start with a fancy cloth-bound empty book. It's too intimidating! It might cause you to worry overmuch about whether you should use a pen rather than a pencil; you could get distressed about your penmanship that has deteriorated with constant use of the computer; filling an expensive journal too quickly may keep you from writing copiously. Just find something inexpensive and get a size that is convenient to carry around with you.
- Write about what is important to you, not about what you think others expect you to write. I schedule two journal discussions during the semester during which I ask students if they wish to share anything from their journals. We talk about the process of journaling and whether or not it is going well. But I never ask them to hand in their journals. I believe it frees people to write deeper reflections if they know they don't have to share it with anyone else.
- Write about what is real to you, what you believe in, what you value. In this way, you may find yourself questioning long-held assumptions.
- Make connections between events and ideas, between actions and reflections, writing about how you feel right then, what your perceptions are at that moment.
- Use your journal to define and solve problems. When you write, try not to have any other distractions. Stay focused. At the same time, if an idea occurs to you while you are engaged in a discussion or in the midst of doing something, take a moment to jot down a note to yourself about it, a few words to trigger reflection when you have time to step back from the press of the day.
- If you like to draw or doodle, add sketches from time to time or diagram your way through an issue. However, be sure to write too, since this gives you a permanent record of the development of your ideas and can help you to communicate them to others.

I encourage you to find a way to make journaling work for you! It could even develop into a lifelong habit that will serve you well as you continue to learn and lead. Both consciously and subconsciously, we reflect on our actions and learn from them. Journaling is a way to fully develop reflection skills and to keep track of your learning.

As I started to write *Leading from Within*, I reflected a great deal upon what I knew about leadership, how I had learned what I knew, and how I practiced both learning and leading. I recalled an incident that occurred when I first began to know myself as a lifelong learner. I remembered taking a philosophy course which began with what I thought was a rather startling announcement. The professor indicated that we were not going to simply **learn about** the philosophy of adult education, we were **going to do** philosophy! And we did! I discovered that it was a very effective way to learn as well as teach. This book is about being a leader, doing leadership. This book is about you! It contains ideas about leading that I wish I had pondered long ago. It is no longer "my" book—it's only reason for existing is for you to make it your book, to fill in the blanks in a way that has meaning for you.

SUMMARY

My continued exploration of theory and models in the leadership literature is valuable to my understanding. However, I am concerned that we may invest too much time trying to find and fit leadership patterns before we discover the path calling us to lead. Just as we don't need to understand the function of all the different pieces of our car or know how to differentiate among all the vehicle makes and models before we begin a journey, we don't need to know everything about leadership before we begin to follow our passion and create positive changes in our community. Being a leader means examining other people's ideas about leadership, but having the courage to create your own model, find your own meaning.

We turn our attention now to a brief discussion of leadership definitions in the next chapter. With the foundation laid for developing a personal frame for your learning and leading, we will delve into the context for change in Chapters 3–5 and then consider how those with a common stake in the outcome might work together for the common good in Chapters 6 and 7.

REFLECTION, APPLICATION, AND RESOURCES

Questions for reflection and journaling:

1. Have you ever called yourself a leader? Has someone else? Describe the circumstances. If you have never seen yourself as a leader, what are the barriers that keep you from leading?

2. How have you learned what you know about leadership? How would you characterize the difference between learning about leadership and learning to be a leader?

Learning activities:

1. On a large piece of paper, list the words that come to mind when you think about leadership. Are some of the words synonyms? If so, rewrite them together and draw a circle or box around them. Next, consider the theoretical point of view suggested by the words you have written. What are the core concepts? How would you design a leadership model from your core concepts? How might your model help others to understand your leadership perspective?

2. Think about people that you recognize as leaders. Make a list of questions that you would like to ask them concerning their leadership role. Here are some sample questions to get you started:

   a. What event or circumstance contributed to your decision to lead?
   b. What guiding principles or philosophical basis guides you as a leader?
   c. What are the most important concepts or skills to know to be effective in your leadership role?
   d. What are the most common mistakes leaders make?

  e. What characterizes truly effective leadership?

  f. Who are some role models who influenced or inspired you? In what ways?

3. Using the questions you developed, interview two leaders and make notes about their responses. How did you choose who to interview? How are they alike and how are they different? If you are studying with a group, compare notes from your interviews. Look for common themes. Develop a group summary concerning the characteristics of effective leaders.

Suggested readings and resources:

1. There are a number of excellent books available on journaling. Three of my favorites are *Life's Companion* by Christina Baldwin, *Writing Down the Bones* by Natalie Goldberg, and Deena Metzger's *Writing for Your Life*.

2. In addition to Rost's *Leadership for the Twenty-First Century* and Bass's update of *Bass and Stodgill's Handbook of Leadership* which are mentioned in the text, J. G. Hunt, in *Leadership: A New Synthesis*, presents a scholarly review of leadership theories, showing the connections to the philosophical assumptions of researchers.

3. Peter Vaill's book, *Learning As a Way of Being*, includes a discussion on perpetual beginners in his second chapter called "Learning As a Way of Being: All Experience is Learning." In particular, see characteristics of a "reflective beginner."

4. Barbara De Angelis has written a delightful little book called *Confidence: Finding It and Living It*. You might find some pearls of wisdom in it as you begin your leadership exploration.

CHAPTER 2

The Meaning of Leadership

The way we learn and practice leadership is changing. Based on my experiences, extensive reading, and intuition, I have a personal sense of some of the changes occurring. This is what shapes my understanding of how we discern leadership's meaning. For example, I have learned from experiencing the stifling weight of heavy-handed leadership which curbs creativity and discourages aspirations. I have also learned from experiencing the nurturing touch of a caring web of collaborative leadership which engages passion and encourages commitment to a community of interest. In this regard, I have made a choice for the latter approach and thus am dedicated to teaching leadership from the heart. My leadership library includes volumes by poets and philosophers, by people in the corporate sector, by teachers and administrators in higher education, by practitioners in community development, by those searching for soul and by devotees of the new science. Intuitively, I am drawn into leadership education because of an innate desire to create a better future in which we might all live and work coupled with the instinctive, optimistic belief that we are all potential leaders in the grand design.

We each have a sense of what leadership or the act of leading means. For each of us, it will be influenced by experience, intuition, our system of values and beliefs, and by what we read and learn about the world around us. In Chapter 2, we will differentiate leading and managing and then focus briefly on some of the definitions of leadership which have evolved over time. The remainder of the chapter deals with the context that influences how leadership is perceived, both generally and personally.

LEADING AND MANAGING

Traditionally, particularly within the corporate sector, we have seen the term leadership applied to the management function where it is historically associated with position and title. In support of those who move up through the bureaucracy, management training programs, which are intended to prepare individuals with the skills necessary to carry out management tasks, are available in abundance. However, the study and practice of leadership, although perhaps incorporating management skills within the context of a leader's mission and goals, has a different focus. This is because managing and leading are not the same. They are different, although not dissociated.

Bennis (1989a), Conger (1992), Vaill (1989), and others have compared management and leadership and offer some insight into what differentiates the two roles. The phrase, "managers do things right, leaders do the right thing" (Bennis, 1989b, p. 18) is a familiar one and offers a broad description.

Administrators are more often managers whereas innovators are leaders. To be a program administrator is to carry out the plans and strategies which are in place within an agency or organization. However, the program leader is the one who conceives the design and perhaps outlines an implementation plan.

Managers focus on structure and methods of control while leaders focus on people and on ways to inspire trust. Often, structure implies hierarchy and how communication must flow up and down through the levels. The concern is for accountability to the next layer up and assuring that a particular unit meets its goals so that other units can attend to their portion of the work. In this way, control of a process or product is supervised. Those who lead are more apt to be concerned with how people relate to each other and to those outside their unit. Additionally, they develop relationships based on the assumption that people know how to do what needs to be done and can be trusted to accomplish goals. Often a manager uses discipline and sanctions to motivate while the leader motivates by creating shared meaning about what work is being done. Leaders often rely on motivation based on intrinsic factors.

Whereas managers have a short-range view and an eye on the bottom line, leaders have a long-range perspective and keep their eyes on the horizon. Deadlines and turnaround time hold the attention of managers, particularly when they concern profits and costs. The leader, however, looks far to the future and sees things from a much broader perspective with less time spent worrying about what needs to be done by the end of the week.

Managers imitate, sticking to what they know about how to do things while leaders originate, dreaming up new ideas and taking more risks. The often used phrase, "If it ain't broke, don't fix it" was probably first spoken by a good manager. In contrast, the newer leadership literature includes a book titled, *If It Ain't Broke, Break It!* (Kriegel & Palter, 1991). This shouldn't be interpreted to mean that leaders are more destructive; however, they are more inclined to try something new before necessity dictates a change. As an illustration, consider early attempts to settle the West. A few brave explorers made the first passage and, once the way was known, others followed. The trailblazers were leaders while managers were in charge of keeping wagon trains to the established path.

A manager is in the habit of taking orders and accepting the status quo. A leader, however is generally his or her own person and often challenges the status quo. For example, in the business world, one often finds that managers do things by the book, following policy and not questioning what is expected of them. Leaders emerge when they begin to question methods, procedures, and policies that have been in place for some time but no longer seem to be appropriate.

In like vein, managers will ask how something should be done and by when, whereas leaders are more concerned with what might be done and why. As mentioned previously, the manager asks, "What's the bottom line?" Other managerial questions might include: "How many do you want and how soon do you need them?" or, "How do you want me to do this?" On the other hand, a leader might ask, "What is possible?" or, "What

if we took a whole different approach?" Perhaps the most significant question leaders ask is simply, "Why?" In this way they
encourage people to be creative and keep the dialogue open.
This synergy, which fosters a spirit of collaboration, produces
innovative results and far-reaching changes.

Managers and leaders have different approaches to change.
Managers play an important role in carrying out changes that
have already been determined. For example, a manager makes
sure appropriate steps are taken to get to a desired future alternative. This is transitional change, accomplished by taking incremental steps in the direction of an anticipated outcome.
Leaders, on the other hand, may well engage a change process
without knowing what the result might be. This intuitive approach is transformative in nature and, more often than not,
includes moving through a period of chaos. Change only happens when we are willing to accept and process new information. A managerial task is to prevent chaos through managing
information. A leader, however, generates information to support the possibility of chaos creating order. Managers want to
reform, focusing on what's wrong and how to fix it. Leaders
want to transform, focusing on what is wanted and how to create it.

Though two separate profiles emerge when comparing
managers and leaders, it should be reiterated that management
and leadership are not mutually exclusive roles. For example,
most effective leaders are well grounded in management concepts. Green (1992) goes so far as to say that management is a
leadership task. All things considered, it is useful to avoid creating a mental dichotomy and to recognize that the distinction
between the two is blurry. Instead, one might think of management and leadership as a continuum with a degree of overlap in
the middle (see Figure 2.1).

Management   Leadership

Figure 2.1 Management—leadership continuum

An Analogy

Another way to understand the relationship between managing and leading is to draw an analogy from anatomy. Each of us has a brain with two distinctly different hemispheres, commonly referred to as left brain and right brain. Each hemisphere takes in information and uses it in a different manner. The left brain is orderly, linear and looks for sequences. The right brain is imaginative, playful, and seeks rhythm and patterns. The logical left brain understands through words while the creative right brain perceives things visually. Fortunately, the two halves of the brain are in constant communication via the corpus callosum which sends impulses back and forth between the hemispheres. Generally, the left brain is the more controlling while the right brain generates new patterns and possibilities. In other words, the right brain thinks up new ideas and things to try and the left brain decides how they might work and puts the process in order.

The analogy suggests that management is a more logical, ordered, left brain undertaking, and that leadership is the more creative, inventive activity. If one thinks about management and leadership as a continuum or as interdependent functions within a group or organization, then staying connected and maintaining communication assure a balance similar to that achieved between the left and right brain. Once again, it is clear that management and leadership are different but not dissociated. For our purposes, however, we will focus primarily on the leadership end of the continuum. Let's turn our attention to how leadership has been defined in the literature.

LEADERSHIP DEFINITIONS

For our purposes, definitions serve as background and provide us with some common understanding. Hughes, Ginnett, and Curphy (1993), Rost (1991), Yukl (1981) and others chronicle definitions of leadership which represent common usage of the term during the last century. They serve to demonstrate the shifting of leadership frames over time and hint at the complex nature of the leadership role. As you consider the list which follows, remember that most of these definitions were developed prior to Bennis's (1989a) work which began to distinguish between leadership and management. Leadership has been defined in the literature as

- The creative and directive force of morale. (Munson, 1921)
- The activity of influencing people to cooperate toward a goal which they come to find desirable. (Tead, 1935)
- The behavior of an individual while involved in directing group activities. (Hemphill, 1949)
- The process of influencing the activities of an organized group in its effort toward goal setting and goal achievement. (Stogdill, 1950)
- The behavior of an individual when directing the activities of a group toward a shared goal. (Hemphill & Coons, 1957)
- The process by which an agent induces a subordinate to behave in a desired manner. (Bennis, 1959)
- Interpersonal influence, exercised in a situation, and directed, through the communication process, toward the attainment of specific goals. (Tannenbaum, Weshler & Massarik, 1961)
- Directing and coordinating the work of group members. (Fiedler, 1967)
- The presence of a particular influence relationship between two or more persons. (Hollander & Julian, 1969)
- The initiation and maintenance of structure in expectation and interaction. (Stogdill, 1974)
- The influential increment over and above mechanical compliance with the routine directives of the organization. (Katz & Kahn, 1978)
- The engagement of others such that leaders and followers transform each other, raising the level of aspiration and morality for purposes which are mutually beneficial. (Burns, 1978)
- The pivotal force behind vital and viable organizations, devel-

oping a new vision of what the organization can be, then mo-
bilizing change toward the new vision. (Bennis & Nanus,
1985)
- Transforming followers, creating visions of the goals that may
  be attained, and articulating for the followers the ways to attain those goals. (Tichy & Devanna, 1986)
- Actions to focus resources to create desirable opportunities.
  (Campbell, 1991)

Over the span of seven decades, we moved from understanding
leadership as a "directive force" to perceiving it in terms of the
use of resources to "create desirable opportunities."

A number of the more recent leadership definitions emphasize the difference between leadership and management as discussed earlier and move toward a view of leadership as a relationship. For example, Kouzes and Posner (1987) not only talk
of the relationship between leader and follower, but state clearly
in their preface that "leadership begins where management ends,
where the systems of rewards and punishments, control and
scrutiny, give way to innovation, individual character, and the
courage of convictions" (p. xvii). More recently, they modify
their definition to say that leadership is a reciprocal relationship
between those who choose to lead and those who choose to follow. Further, the authors claim that the key to unlocking greater
leadership potential can be found only when one understands
the service relationship (Kouzes & Posner, 1993). Wheatley
(1992), in speaking of leadership as a relationship, holds that
leadership is the willingness to stay and the capacity to connect.
Rost (1991) echoes the description of leadership as a relationship and urges us to think of leadership as a communal relationship. He makes clear his perspective on the parameters of leadership in his definition: "Leadership is an influence relationship
among leaders and followers who intend real changes that reflect
their mutual purposes (p. 102)." This definition of leadership is
widely regarded by the academic community as comprehensive
and yet specific enough to be used in leadership research. We
will explore leadership as a relationship in Chapter 6.

CONTEXT INFLUENCES MEANING

For many of us whose interest in leadership tends toward the practical application rather than research and study, definitions are useful, but may not encompass the richness of meaning we have experienced. Definitions set boundaries whereas meaning is concerned with significance and making sense. We each come to our own intuitive definition of leadership through learning and leading in a relevant context. It is the context which shapes the meaning of leadership. There is a great deal happening in communities and organizations that is shaping the way leadership is understood. Some of those influences include changes in how power is viewed, interest in the servant leadership philosophy, quantum physics as a metaphor for describing organizations, application of total quality management in organizational development, and efforts to create learning organizations.

Power in the Leadership Relationship

The notion of leadership as a relationship signals a dramatic shift in understanding the association between power and leadership. Rather than conceiving of power in terms of hierarchical structures and tangible resources (power over), more and more organizations are engaging human resources to manage processes and information (power with). "Power is ethically neutral. It can be used for good purposes or bad" (Gardner, 1990, p. 66). Power is about our capacity to do things and this capacity can only be developed with others. Leaders and collaborators share the power within and through their organization to produce true change. Both see power as never being completely one way, but as a relationship (Earnest, 1994). Apps, in *Leadership for the Emerging Age* (1994), describes a paradox: the more power a leader gives away, the more power the leader has. But it is a different kind of power. It is the power of shared information, of dialogue, and eventually, of transformation.

Servant Leadership

Servant leadership, a relatively new philosophical perspective, was introduced in the early seventies and is currently gaining a foothold in the corporate sector. The Greenleaf Center in Indianapolis, whose mission is to improve the caring quality of institutions through servant leadership, was named in honor of the late Robert K. Greenleaf, originator of the concept of servant leadership. His ideas are useful in clarifying the relationship between leader and follower that exists within each of us. People neither lead all the time nor follow all the time. Leaders who share power and create an environment which nurtures collaboration may occasionally find themselves partnering with their employees on a work project. In essence, the leader chooses to be a follower in certain contexts and, at the same time, expects followers to step into the role of leader as the situation warrants. Servant leaders have a common purpose—to replace competition with community. Servant leadership is a walk of faith which transforms leaders and followers who recognize that coping isn't the only answer. It is grounded in a way of leading which, rather than telling people what to do, gives meaning to what they are already doing (Spears, 1995).

Quantum Physics Metaphor

Recent discoveries in the sciences, especially physics, have found application in understanding organizations today. The movement from characterizing organizations as machines to perceiving them as organic systems parallels the thinking undergirding the shift from Newtonian physics to quantum physics (see Figure 2.2). Quantum physics and chaos theory have sparked ideas about organizations that have shaken historical and familiar ideas about rationality as the guiding law of all decisions. The western world's mechanistic perspective does not leave room for human nature, resulting in a worldview in which we can no longer find ourselves—as humans or as organizations. We think of chaos as the antithesis of all we strive for in our

Summary of Contrasting Characteristics	
Newtonian	**Quantum**
Certainty	Uncertainty
Continuous	Discontinuous
Linear	Nonlinear
Reductionist	Creative
Isolated	Contextual
Hierarchical	Nonhierarchical
Either/Or	Both/And
Actuality	Potentiality

Figure 2.2 Physics metaphor

lives. However, when we discover ourselves in the midst of chaos, there are those who would point out to us that chaos seeks order in much the same way that life itself is system-seeking (Wheatley, 1992).

Seeing organizations as systems rather than machines leads us to recognize a shift in how we describe the role of leader. The Newtonian organizational scheme requires people in positions of authority whose task is to exercise power and control behaviors as people move along an incremental path of change. This approach does not fare well in the quantum organization which is characterized by collaborative leadership and shared power. There is a continuous effort to create meaning and pursue ideas which have potential for changes which may not even be clear initially. Wheatley (1992) would go so far as to say that one can never direct a human system, one can only disturb it!

Total Quality Management

The Total Quality Management (TQM) movement has had a profound effect on changing the shape and focus of corporations, organizations, and government institutions. TQM is a practical, strategic approach to managing an organization which focuses on the needs of its customers and clients. The intent is to reject any outcome other than excellence (Sallis, 1993). It in-

```
┌─────────────────────────────────────────────────────┐
│  TQM CORE CONCEPTS AND VALUES                         │
│                                                       │
│  Customer-driven quality                              │
│  Leadership                                           │
│  Continuous improvement                               │
│  Employee participation and development               │
│  Fast response                                        │
│  Design quality and prevention                        │
│  Long-range outlook                                   │
│  Management by fact                                   │
│  Partnership development                              │
│  Corporate responsibility and development             │
└─────────────────────────────────────────────────────┘
```

Figure 2.3 Deming's TQM principles (*Adapted from Schmidt & Finnigan, 1992*)

vokes a way of operating (see Figure 2.3) that incorporates ten core concepts and values developed by Deming (Schmidt & Finnigan, 1992).

TQM has changed the way in which managers function. To be effective in an organization which has embraced Deming's ideas, it must empower rather than control people, using methods such as training and coaching rather than directing and supervising. Collaboration is encouraged over competition within the organization and so leaders must develop new policies designed to recognize and reward the team effort. They emphasize improvement rather than maintenance, developing systems that support the quality effort and improve communication. Instead of quality inspection at the end of the production line, the process itself is scrutinized. When processes are changed, the organization is transformed. Thus, although the term management figures prominently in this approach, implications for leadership are manifested as well.

Learning Organizations

Another growing influence on how organizations will function in the future comes from the idea that they have the capacity to learn. Senge (1990) introduced the concept of learning organizations, an outgrowth of systems thinking. His five "disciplines" of a learning organization are personal mastery, mental models, shared vision, team learning, and systems thinking. Personal mastery is about individual awareness and openness to change. Mental models are assumptions, those preconceived notions by which we operate that we must be willing to examine, and perhaps discard, because they limit new thinking and growth. Shared vision goes beyond simple acceptance of a lofty statement coming from the top, to building a common sense of purpose. Team learning carries the vision forward as people work together to achieve a sense of community. The fifth discipline, systems thinking, is about getting a "big picture" perspective of an organization, seeing beyond the details, and understanding the dynamic complexity. Systems thinking is a way of engaging organizational challenges by seeking out root causes. Its foundation rests on the principle that the stakeholders already have within them both the creativity and the wisdom, to confront through dialogue, even the most difficult challenges.

The process undertaken by a learning organization is cyclic (Senge, Roberts, Ross, Smith, & Kleiner, 1994) and involves an investment of time (see Figure 2.4). Individuals (the inner circle) are encouraged to reflect upon what goes on within the organization and search out connections among people, ideas, and processes. Time spent in mental exploration then sets the stage for making new plans and carrying them out. The cycle begins again when implementation of the plan is considered and evaluated, fostering new connections, and so on.

Within an organization (the outer circle), the language changes slightly to incorporate multiple perspectives—public reflection, shared meaning, joint planning, and coordinated action. Reflecting and connecting are time consuming and do not produce the tangible results expected from the planning and doing stages of the learning cycle. Organizational leaders may need to establish a significant shift in mind-set to engage the development of a true learning organization. The way we learn and practice leadership is changing. From my perspective, the creation and cultivation of learning organizations produces exem-

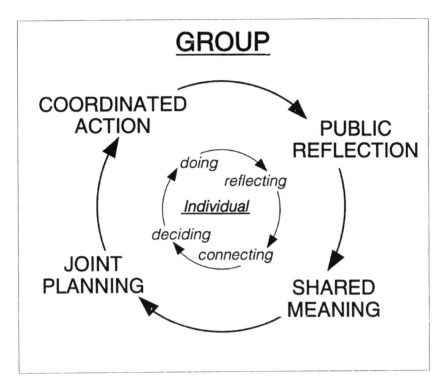

Figure 2.4 Organization Learning Cycle (*Adapted from Senge et al., 1994*)

plary models which transform the meaning of leadership while transforming the organization.

SUMMARY

Both organizational and personal definitions of leadership are modified in keeping with our contextual experiences, our reading and reflection. Change is the constant theme. As community and organizational contexts change and as we experience change, the meaning of leadership changes. Who we are while we are learning and leading changes. Others' definitions are adapted as the meaning of leadership is personalized and clarified for each of us. For me, leadership is a shared responsibility for creating a better world in which to live and work. It is manifested in our passion to engage others in bringing about purposeful change.

Only a few have been presented in this chapter, but leadership definitions are plentiful. While most of the recent definitions clearly distinguish between leadership and management, those presented early in the literature often used the terms synonymously. For our purposes, these definitions serve as background and provide us with some common understanding. Each one describes leadership in its own way, within its own context. This is a starting point for creating personal meaning.

Ask yourself—how does leadership manifest itself in your life? This is where you will discover its meaning. When you started reading this chapter, you already had some ideas about leadership, but did you see yourself in that mental picture? Defining leadership for yourself is contingent upon, in fact shaped by, your own reason for leading, the issues which move you to take the lead, and the context within which all this happens. The next chapter explores the purpose of leadership.

REFLECTION, APPLICATION, AND RESOURCES

Questions for reflection and journaling:

1. How do you see yourself as a leader? What do you do when you are leading? What is your definition of leadership?

2. To what extent are your answers to these questions shaped by your environment—place of work, the club you belong to, the organization of which you are a part?

3. Think about the two leaders you interviewed in the exercise at the end of the previous chapter. Where would you place them on the management-leadership continuum in Figure 2.1? Why?

Learning activities:

1. Using lots of colored marking pens and a big sheet of paper (newsprint works well if you have it available), draw a picture, symbol, or diagram that represents what leadership means to you. Avoid using words! Don't worry about the level of your artistic ability. This is about symbolism, not about drawing. Keep your picture someplace where you can look at it again later and reflect on it from time to time. If you are working in a group, complete the above exercise and then share your drawings, allowing time for each person to describe and explain his or her symbol. During the discussion, listen for common themes and develop a group list of leadership characteristics.

2. Look through five or six leadership books that are of interest to you. Find each author's definition of leadership and compare it to your own.

Suggested readings and resources:

1. If you are interested in learning more about quantum physics, see Fritjof Capra's early book called *The Tao of Physics* or, more recently, Margaret Wheatley's *Leadership and the New Science*.

2. TQM applications in higher education is the focus of a book by Cornesky called *Using Deming to Improve Quality in Colleges and Universities*. Schmidt and Finnigan have written *TQManager* to support the efforts of individuals in any organization that has adopted a TQM strategy. For practical applications, see *The Team Handbook* by Peter Scholtes.

3. Senge's *The Fifth Discipline* is the cornerstone of current writing about learning organizations. *The Fifth Discipline Fieldbook*, by Senge et al. is the practical companion book. I also suggest *Sculpting the Learning Organization* by Watkins and Marsick.

4. For information on right-brain and left-brain thinking, see Williams and Stockmyer's *Unleashing the Right Side of the Brain* or Buzan's *Use Both Sides of Your Brain.*

5. Nancy Margulies has written a wonderful book called *Mapping Inner Space* which can get you started doing and teaching mind mapping, a creative technique for exploring relationships among words and ideas.

CHAPTER 3

A Reason for Leading

Leadership without purpose has no meaning. The fallacy of many leadership development programs and classes is that they are not grounded in a particular context. This struck me when, after a decade of leadership development programming in rural communities and with organizations and agencies, I turned my attention to teaching leadership in a college classroom. As I worked through the first few weeks of an experimental course called Leadership Concepts and Contexts, it became apparent that something was missing. Quite frankly, my first attempt to offer the course was floundering. When I analyzed the situation, I discovered a major difference between what I was trying to do in the classroom setting and what had been successful in my previous work. Developing a leadership education program for a community group that was interested in providing leadership for a river ecology awareness effort was not the same as teaching an interdisciplinary course to students who came together from a variety of backgrounds and expectations. Whereas community members were focused on their shared intent, the classroom was simply a group of students who were curious about leadership.

I began to consider some alternatives that I hoped might energize my teaching and provide some direction for the students. I wanted them to feel a sense of excitement about their own capacity to lead. What was it that I believed about leadership that was so important? How would the things that I valued about leadership serve as a guide for how I taught my students and tapped their potential to lead? After much reflection and soul-searching, it was clear to me that what was missing was a personal sense of purpose, individually or collectively, to give meaning to the process of learning leadership. Each time I had been asked to bring leadership education to a community or an organization, the individuals involved had already known why they wanted to learn to lead.

It was time to change. I would need to let go of the way I had been teaching about leadership and engage students in being leaders, doing leadership. We could begin by taking stock together and celebrating what they already knew about leadership. At the same time, I recognized that modeling what I believed about shared leadership meant "giving away" the syllabus and involving everyone in designing the remaining classes to maximize the potential for each of them to find their own inner meaning within a context that was personally relevant. My experience with both teaching and learning, guided by my working philosophy of nonformal education, helped me decide to facilitate their learning rather than simply teach about leadership.

Together, we took action. Since it was too late in the semester to develop a group project to provide the parameters for what they wanted to learn, we began to probe beyond their general curiosity about leadership to get to their personal passion. As they began to realize what they cared about enough to want to change, we worked on vision and mission statements. We talked about leadership strategies. We developed matrices for exploring the issues about which they were concerned. Although we ran out of time before we could meet everyone's objectives for skill development within their own context, the students had gained an understanding of the means and methods to continue their growth as leaders. At the end of the semester, we evaluated what had happened. As I reflected on their suggestions and my analysis of this first attempt to take leadership development into the classroom, I began to see the transformation that would change my teaching forever. Learning leadership is about a personal context for change.

LEADERSHIP FOR CHANGE

The story of how my leadership education program was transformed illustrates how seeing an opportunity for change engages us in leading. Coping with the program as it was just wasn't good enough. I cared too much to accept the status quo even though I knew I was employing all the standard methods and using appropriate resources. Change was necessary if I wanted to offer something more than information about what others thought leadership meant in practice. In this chapter, we will discuss change and how it is the foundation of one's leadership purpose. Creating a personal vision for the changes you intend is a way for you to understand your leadership purpose and reflect your intent to those you wish to engage in the process of bringing about the desired changes.

The simplest reason for leadership is change. Whether you want to lead an effort to secure more books for your rural library, to bring about a stronger sense of community on your campus or build a network of artists for world harmony, your internal motivation is to bring about change. When you care enough to want to make a difference, you are poised to learn and practice leadership. However, experience has probably taught you that change isn't always an easy process and that different people have different responses to it.

Change has been studied for years and there is still much to discover. It is a complex notion and continues to evolve. Even the nature of change is changing according to noted author Charles Handy. "Change is not what it used to be," he declares (1989, p. 6). In a like vein, Anderson (1990) says that things change, and the way things change changes. The speed and complexity of change in the emerging age often surpass our ability to understand its nature. This all seems a bit esoteric if we choose to leave the responsibility for change to those in positions of power.

Many of us have been in situations where change was something that happened to us rather than a process that we initiated or had any means for moderating. For example, changes in policy or structure where we work are often launched by people in higher positions who are reacting to external pressures. But this is not always the case. Time and again I have seen far-reaching changes started by someone in a work group or on a committee who believed that there must be a better way. In the previous chapter, I presented several ideas that are influencing how people think about change in organizations or in communities. Senge (1990) describes the more traditional view as one based on powerlessness in which people look to a few great leaders to do for them what they can't do for themselves. The evolving paradigm, however, holds that individuals are taking responsibility for building organizations by increasing their capacity for understanding complexity and by learning to involve others in bringing about change. This personal sense of purpose is the premise upon which learning organizations (discussed in the previous chapter) are built.

Dissatisfaction with the status quo is the catalyst which moves us toward taking responsibility for change. You may desire to modify the power structure where you work, create more opportunity for people in your community, increase the possibility of personal growth among family or friends, or change any situation you believe can be better. The magnitude of the change depends on the context within which it is desired and the effort invested by leaders and followers.

THREE TYPES OF CHANGE

Although many people view ANY change as a major upheaval, there are three types of change which characterize varying degrees of turmoil within a community or organization— incremental, transitional, and transformational. Expectations of leaders are likely to be different for each type of change.

Incremental change is the gradual, developmental change which happens over an unspecified time. It is change which takes place when improvements are made. For example, early calculators were cumbersome, slow, expensive, and not widely used. Over time, design and technology improved. Now they are commonplace, modestly priced, very efficient, and come in a range of sizes, some not much larger than a credit card. Just as improvements may be made in a product, so does developmental change occur when a process is improved. This is what the quality movement mentioned in the previous chapter is designed to do. For instance, finding ways to decrease the amount of time it takes to sort and deliver mail at your local post office is an example of process improvement. The function of the leader in incremental change situations may be to manage the team that is working to improve the process or the product, monitor progress, encourage open exchange of ideas, and keep morale at a high level.

Transitional change occurs when the anticipated outcome is known. If you were to begin at point A (the current situation) and head for point B (the desired state), transitional change is about taking care of what lies between the two points. Implementation of this type of change concerns the management of the interim state over a predetermined period of time. As an illustration, if the grocery store where you shop decided to add an on-site bakery, implementing the transition could easily include disruptions that affect parking, increased noise while you shop as carpenters do their work, temporary shelving in unexpected places as grocery items are moved to accommodate construction, and so on. Similarly, store employees may experience these same inconveniences and others related to communication breakdowns and temporary changes in their work assignments. Thus, even though the change is a positive one and eagerly anticipated, the change process can cause confusion and unpleasantness. It is no wonder that people resist change—the transition can be very difficult! The role of the leader in bringing about transitional change may involve articulating the vision, marketing the new concept both internally and externally, managing damage control, keeping people on schedule, and planning for a celebration when the transition has been accomplished.

Transformational change is characteristically unpredictable. Chaos is produced by a trigger event, often emerging either from the fringes of an organization or from external factors, instead of being initiated by those in established positions of power. The outcomes of transformational change cannot be discerned until the process is well underway. Consider, for example, the unstable conditions in many social service agencies following a round of budget cuts thrust upon them by a conservative legislature. This sort of event makes it immediately clear that things will change, but just how the agency will operate

under these new constraints is not known at the outset. However, it is not uncommon for an agency so affected to come
through the transformation process stronger, more focused, and
clearer about its mission. The difference between an organization that brings about a successful transformation and one that
merely survives after a trigger event (such as a severe budget cut)
lies in how its leadership approaches the change process. Coping
with change is a passive tactic and one that spells defeat. Engaging the process and getting involved in creating desirable change
from undesirable circumstances is an energizing strategy that
makes for a vibrant organization. Leadership in a transformation process can come from anywhere in the organization and
is a shared responsibility. These leaders must be able to sustain
a dialogue, maintain optimism, be creative and engender a climate that encourages others to be creative, integrate a wide variety of perspectives, and invest time in developing shared meaning among those who have a stake in the transformation.

THE TRANSFORMATION CYCLE

In the example just mentioned, drastic budget cuts have
spawned a profusion of dramatic changes since the middle of the
last decade, most notably among publicly funded organizations.
One such case is that of the Cooperative Extension Service, the
educational system serving the agricultural community and rural areas nationwide. In response to diminishing resources, the
National Extension Leadership Development (NELD) program
was designed to assist administrators and emerging leaders in
meeting the challenge of bringing about the transformation
of the organization. NELD's creator and first director, Jerold
Apps, developed a model to explain the process of transformation (see Figure 3.1).

The initial phase of the transformation cycle begins with
awareness and analysis of current reality. Questions to ask include "What's going well?" and "What's not going well?" This
is followed by exploration of possible alternatives to the current

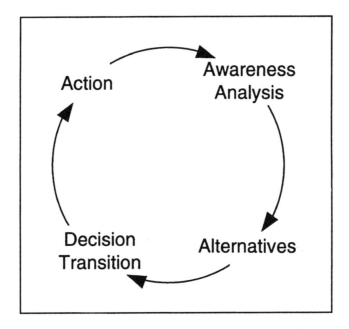

Figure 3.1 Transformation cycle (*from Apps, 1992, p. 1*)

situation. This stage can be time-consuming and involve reading, discussion with associates and others with experience in the same type of arena, and assessment of values and beliefs. Next, it is time to decide what to do and initiate the transition. This phase of transformation may be gut-wrenching, characterized by mourning the loss of old ways of thinking and operating while celebrating a new direction. Once a decision is made and plans for the transition are underway, action follows as the next step. Doing what it takes to bring about thoughtful change energizes individuals as well as organizations. However, it is necessary to reflect on those actions and the cycle begins again.

The cycle is as applicable to each person and each leader as it is to an organization. In addition, the process described parallels Senge's model for how organizations learn presented in the second chapter. In the past, you may have thought about yourself (or your organization) as learning to adapt to change. The intent of this book, to engage you in learning that is designed to evoke change, is reflected in the transformation cycle.

A VISION OF A PREFERRED FUTURE

Take a moment to consider your objectives for choosing to read *Leading from Within*. Perhaps your response includes reasons such as curiosity about what leaders do, a desire to stand out among your peers, or a wish to be more skillful in combating your foe(s). Perhaps the book is required reading for some course. I believe it is because you can see yourself leading. What does that look like? Do you have a personal vision, one that is powerful enough to compel you to lead? Do you want your existence on earth to have made a difference? When you can see in your mind's eye the results of the changes you want to bring about, you have a vision of a preferred future.

At this point, my right brain is asking me to invite you to play, to be creative, to imagine a whole host of possibilities. At the same time, my left brain is saying that this should be a logical process and there must be a sequence of steps to achieve a compelling vision. Yes! Both kinds of thinking are involved. It has been said that a vision statement is both a dream and a road map (Apps, 1990).

A place to begin is to assess your current situation. The process I suggest for your vision and mission work is similar to one in which I participated a number of years ago. It was introduced by Michael Brazzel who was, at that time, on the federal staff for the Cooperative Extension System. Since that time, David Sanderson and I have adapted it for use with a regional leadership project which he helped me to facilitate. And the process continues to evolve. To begin, you will want to consider what's going well and what isn't with respect to the following:

Behavior—what you do and don't do along with how you do it.

Thinking—how you find meaning in incoming information (your thoughts, attitudes, values, world view).

Feeling—what goes on in your emotional life (anger, fear, joy, and so on).

Body—current health state, fitness, the way you take care of yourself, habits.

Spirit—your sense of your soul, the core of your being and its relationship to a source of power outside yourself.

Anything else—relationships, work, family, leisure, income, possessions, education, and so on.
(Note: An organization can begin a visioning exercise with some modifications of this same set of questions.)

I find it helpful to take a blank sheet of paper, draw a line down the middle, label one side WHAT'S GOING WELL and the other, WHAT'S NOT GOING WELL. As I begin to make a list, I often move back and forth between columns. You may find, as I did, that the "not going well" side is easier to generate. That's all right—sometimes we just need to look at negatives a bit differently to turn them into something more positive. Being able to see things from a different perspective is the hallmark of creativity.

Take time to reflect on your two lists. First, make sure you have been honest with yourself. Then, imagine what you would like to list in the "going well" column. What are your hopes and dreams? Is there perhaps a theme that emerges, several items that are interconnected? How could the things that are going well be even better?

Now you should be ready to begin writing your vision statement. Your vision statement is the deepest expression of what you truly want. It is grounded in the belief that you have the right and responsibility to create yourself according to your own desires and values and that you become what you envision. You are writing a word picture for a preferred future, a desired state that is a leap from where you are today. It is operational and real: a portrayal of what you really want to be. Your vision statement should be exciting, motivating, compelling, and almost embarrassingly lofty! It should engage the spirit and capture the imagination, moving you toward what you choose to be. Here are some guidelines for creating your vision statement:

- Focus on the result of what you truly want for yourself (or your organization), not on the immediate steps for getting there.
- Separate what you truly want from what you think is possible. A vision is about what you really want.
- Focus on what you want, not on what you don't want.
- Make choices for yourself—not for other people or organizations.
- Express your vision in the present tense rather than the future, for example "I am . . . " rather than "I will be . . . " and "We are . . . " rather than "We strive to become . . . "
- Keep it short, specific, and concrete.

Embedded in your vision, you will find clues concerning why you want to lead, what it is that you really would like to change. Learning leadership will then become purposeful for you. "At the heart of leadership is a fundamental question, 'Leadership for what?'. . . . Perhaps the most important elements of leadership turn on the question, 'Leadership for what?' " (Green, 1992, p. 68). Position and title are not the starting point. Your passion for the preferred future you envision will provide you with the basic credentials necessary for learning and leading. It is the catalyst that implores you to explore leadership concepts, probe your personal issue and its context, affirm your values and beliefs, develop collaborative relationships, and then learn appropriate skills necessary to bring about the positive change envisioned.

SUMMARY

The overarching purpose of leadership is change. In this chapter, we have briefly explored three types of change and considered how a transformation cycle describes the nature of the changes we intend. Then, in the spirit of doing rather than simply learning about, you have been asked to create a personal leadership vision. Being a leader means caring enough about something to want to make a difference. Doing leadership means being able to articulate your vision for change.

Your reason for leading sets the parameters for the work you will do through the rest of *Leading from Within*. In Chapter 4 we will begin to explore what lies within those parameters— your context for leading.

REFLECTION, APPLICATION, AND RESOURCES

Questions for reflection and journaling:

1. Think about changes in your life that you feel were significant. List several and then choose one that really stands out in your mind. What were the circumstances that brought about this change? How did you feel when it happened? How would you characterize the change—incremental, transitional, or transformational? Was it something you caused to happen? If so, what did you do? If it wasn't of your own doing, how did you react?

2. Leadership is about change. What change or changes are you in the process of bringing about? What would you like to change? Can you think of some specific instances when you decided that coping was not the solution?

Learning activities:

1. My story at the beginning of this chapter is an example of how the transformation cycle played out in real life. Read through it once more and look for the various stages of transformation.

2. After you have done an initial assessment and are ready to begin creating your vision statement, brainstorm as many ideas as you can for your vision. Jot them down on sticky notes, one thought per note. Work quickly and be brief. When you have finished, paste all the notes on a large sheet of newsprint and read them through. Rearrange them into groups of related ideas and, over each group, write headers such as career, relationships, ecology, and so on. You may be

surprised at what emerges. To complete the exercise, review each group and, using the visioning guidelines in this chapter, construct one sentence that captures the essence of each grouping. I often use this technique when working with a small organization with all participants contributing ideas and then developing summary statements for each header in small groups.

3. Imagine that you have lived a long and full life and have accomplished many things. Now, imagine that you are the journalist assigned to write your obituary. Describe yourself as you would like to be remembered.

Suggested readings and resources:

1. See Larraine Matusak's recent book, *Finding Your Voice: Learning to Lead Anywhere You Want to Make a Difference.* On page 22, she presents a very useful exercise for discovering what issues are important to you.

2. On pages 150 to 159 in Senge's *Fifth Discipline*, there is a wonderful discussion of creative tension which may be helpful as you work on developing a clear understanding of your current reality and its relationship to your vision.

3. Weisbord's "Four-Room Apartment" that he uses for determining readiness for change in an organization is discussed on pages 266–271 in his book, *Productive Workplaces.*

4. Greenleaf talks about "marker events," those things that happen in our lives which are critical turning points. These very often are the beginning places for learning and leading. Recommended reading includes *The Servant As Leader*, and *On Becoming a Servant Leader.*

CHAPTER 4

The Context for Leading

Not long after she moved to Arizona, my sister realized that the work she had always loved and that seemed a natural fit for her personality and talent was no longer satisfying. Becoming a different person wasn't the issue—she wanted to become who she really was inside. Mary had been an emergency medical technician and then a dispatcher for an urban medical emergency agency for many years. She took pride in her ability to analyze complex situations, respond quickly, and provide competent, caring service to people in need. However, she found herself longing to be able to apply that talent in a way which helped people make positive, planned changes in their lives rather than simply be a caregiver in response to a dramatic, life-threatening event. It was time to change. In fact, it was time to be a change agent rather than a support person helping people cope with changes.

She envisioned a personal future which involved leading others to better health through natural and holistic methods. She decided to explore alternative health care, specifically massage therapy. Her assessment of her current reality sparked a purposeful examination of the environment in which she hoped to be working and a number of questions emerged. What could she learn about her chosen field? What new skills would she need and how could she develop them? How would she manage her own business? Eventually she would need equipment and supplies—what did that entail? Where would she get them? Who else was practicing massage therapy in her community? Did the American Massage Therapy Association have an active local chapter? What were the prevailing theories concerning massage therapy? What was her position relative to the varying philosophies? When should she start course work in massage therapy? What was available locally? Did she have the resources for the changes she would make? How would she face her fears and minimize the risks? Given all the changes in store, what was her mission to be?

Mary knew that, at some point, she would go back to school to learn the specific skills and concepts necessary for her choice to become a massage therapist. However, she also knew that there was a great deal she must learn and discover on her own. She would, in essence, be her own teacher, learning as she probed the context of what was emerging as her new reality.

CONTEXT OVERVIEW

Mary's story is about context—grounding her newly envisioned purpose in the particular setting where changes were to take place. Once she examined her alternatives and made a decision about her purpose for leading, the context for change provided the backdrop for determining her course of action. A vision for change is not insulated from what goes on in the environment in which it is anchored. In reality, there is a mutual dependence. The context includes vision, mission, and the situation—what is going on and who is involved. In this chapter, we will explore not only our personal context for change, but who we are and what we do within that context.

Uncovering information about the various elements of the context and understanding what it means will take time. But it is time well invested since hopes and plans can quickly go awry without sufficient knowledge of the milieu surrounding intended change. This is true whether you are inviting change into your own life, introducing change within an organization, or invoking the transformation of an entire system. There is no template for context, no set approach for discovering what is important, and no succinct definition. Each context is different depending on our vision for change. We worked though a visioning process in the previous chapter. It is time to turn our attention to developing a mission statement.

DEVELOPING A MISSION STATEMENT

The vision statement you worked on in the previous chapter was about what compels you to lead. It answers the question, "Why?" Your mission statement is about what you do and how your effort moves in the direction of your vision. A mission statement is about identity and purpose. It describes what it is that an organization or group does or, on a personal level, the reason for being. We can begin to write a mission statement by simply listing the things we do. For clues, look back through the work we've already done. In our assessment of what is going well and what isn't, we enumerate actions that describe what we do. Our purpose for leading and the vision we have of the changes we wish to create are all linked to what we do and how we will bring about the intended changes.

A list, however, is not a mission statement. How can this list become the framework which guides our actions, the lens through which we see ourselves accomplishing what we set out to do? Check first to make sure the initial list isn't simply a compilation of accomplishments. A mission should not simply reiterate the goals and objectives you have achieved. Instead, look for the meaning behind your actions and consider what you want to be doing. What does your vision tell you about what you want to be doing, your purpose for leading? What is central to your mission?

A clear and effective mission statement will have the following characteristics.

A mission statement

- describes the core function, what you are all about, your reason for being without which your life would have no meaning, the thing you do uniquely well, the purpose that justifies your being;
- includes the one critical purpose rather than the trivial many;
- is brief so that it can be easily recalled;
- is a living document which is reviewed regularly and revised when appropriate;
- is concrete and easy to understand rather than abstract;

- identifies expectations of and intentions toward others—followers, staff, customers, the public, and so on;
- is a means for aligning what you SAY you do with what you actually do, and with what others believe is your purpose;
- is a tool which establishes broad, overall direction for your leadership and your touchstone for making key decisions;
- clarifies what you are NOT trying to do and who you are NOT trying to be; and
- is visible, communicated, and remembered.

As you finish writing your personal mission statement, read through the characteristics just described to see if you have covered all of the important elements. Then as a final check, compare your vision and your mission. The vision should express your highest hopes, a dream for the future that compels you to lead. The mission is a framework for action, a map to chart your journey toward achieving your purpose.

An example of a personal mission statement might read something like this:

> My mission is to help my organization and the individuals within it to become more self-directed, collaborative, and productive as we create a sense of community in our workplace.

Once you begin to think about mission statements, you will begin to see them more frequently. There may be one hanging on the wall where you rent a vehicle, another somewhere in the brochure you receive from a local charity during its annual fund drive, and others when you visit most any corporate web site. The following example of an organizational mission statement is drawn from the National Coastal Resources Institute (NCRI):

> NCRI is committed to promoting American economic growth and prosperity by engaging partnerships that move research and technology into action to improve the economic well-being of the nation's coastal communities, the competitiveness of coastal business, and the quality of life of all citizens.

Each of these examples represents a clearly articulated reason for being. It is important to remember that neither your vision nor your mission exists in a vacuum. Who you are as a leader is inexorably intertwined with the situation in which you are leading, the context in which you intend to bring about changes.

THE SITUATION

Context includes much more than mission and vision. The exploration continues as we assess what is going on in the environment that will influence the intended change. What is it about the situation that must be understood so that leadership efforts will result in the change envisioned? It involves other people, the activities in which they are engaged, various organizations and agencies, and history and culture relevant to the intended change. Our whole environment contributes to the contextual milieu. There are forces at work within the context that can either inhibit or enhance our change effort.

Unfortunately, I don't know any set formula for investigating and analyzing context that is universal. The process involves research, active learning, intuition, drudgery, question framing, problem solving, and luck, all coming together to make sense for you. After I wrote Mary's story at the beginning of this chapter, I read it to her to see if I had accurately portrayed what happened. After all, she was allowing me to use her as an example and I didn't want to write anything that didn't feel right for her. Her comment was, "You made it sound a lot smoother than it felt!" Probing your context may feel awkward and unwieldy, but don't be discouraged. I do know a place where you can begin your own context exploration and I can offer some suggestions that might help.

SELF-AWARENESS

Put yourself in your context first. The process of self-assessment is ongoing, sometimes purposeful, sometimes instinctive. It is purposeful when we consciously ask ourselves questions in an effort to adjust our behavior or to check the accuracy of our thinking processes. For example, when we see that it is a cloudy morning, we ask ourselves whether we should prepare for a rainy day. Perhaps we respond by getting an umbrella from the closet or by deciding to drive to work rather than ride a bicycle. On the other hand, when we realize that we're making mistakes on the keyboard because our fingers feel stiff and cold, our bodies have instinctively made an assessment of the temperature and, finding the room chilly, have triggered some action. We adjust the thermostat or pull on a sweater.

As the process of self-assessment begins within the context of the change we are trying to bring about, most of that activity will be carried out consciously, tapping body, mind, and spirit—the whole self. Values, attitudes, assumptions, and beliefs will be brought to the surface for thorough examination. Behaviors that will enhance the change process will be identified and those that may inhibit will be scrutinized, to be modified when feasible and appropriate. Often, this means seeking out and listening openly to others who know us well and who are willing to provide honest input concerning what we really do and how it affects others. It may even lead to seeking out someone who doesn't know us well to observe and clarify our behaviors. Self-awareness includes assessing our talents. We need to ask what we bring to the changes we envision and be alert to what skills we need to learn to be successful. Throughout this assessment, the vision for change to which we aspire will serve as a touchstone, a guiding light as we home in on clarifying just what our mission is.

Intuitive knowledge should not be overlooked in the process. Listening skills are important when we are seeking information from others. They are just as important when we assess what goes on deep in our innermost self. Different listening skills are needed for this assessment. It involves listening to that still, small voice inside us which instinctively knows what is good, to those gut feelings that can't be wrong, to the song of serendipity that wells up from our hearts, and to that central core which carries our souls' purpose. When we tap intuitive knowledge, listen deeply, and trust, then we become fully attuned to ourselves. Since you are a key person within your context, this deep self-knowledge is essential in developing your understanding of that context.

To enhance the introspective self-assessment, I encourage the use of some type of personal preference inventory. There are many instruments available although a large proportion of them focus more specifically on business setting applications. The two I have found most useful are the Myers-Briggs Type Indicator (Myers, 1962) and the Personal Profile System.

The MBTI is widely used. Since many of those with whom I work have already discovered their Myers-Briggs type, I have been using the Personal Profile System for more than a decade. Adding the Personal Profile System to what you may have learned about yourself from the MBTI adds a new perspective and deepens self-awareness. You can do the Personal Profile assessment individually and work through several informative exercises in the booklet. However, if you and others in your group are willing to share your profiles, there is a great deal that can be learned from discussion and interaction. A group setting allows for exploration of the pros and cons of each of the preferred patterns of behavior and affirms that there is no "best" profile or pattern. Information in the assessment booklet outlines each pattern's emotions, fears, goals, ways of judging others, and ways of influencing people, and then offers suggestions for how to increase personal effectiveness.

You are encouraged to make use of a personal assessment tool as you continue your learning journey. As awareness of your own preferred way of operating is heightened, you become more aware of others' behavior as well. This enhances self-understanding and contributes to the development of leadership capacity. With a clearer sense of who you are within your context, we turn now to delving into the rest of the process.

THE PROBING PROCESS

My left brain keeps searching for the logical sequence of steps involved in examining the context. But my right brain insists that this is a generative process and will happen because you will discover the patterns and linkages that make sense for you. Applying the whole brain would seem to involve both approaches, creatively generating your own logic through inductive reasoning. The process may involve a variety of methods: information gathering, data analysis, brainstorming, reflecting, engaging in dialogue (perhaps with yourself as well as with others), creating alternative future scenarios, assessing, building linkages, imagining, sorting, discarding, challenging, clarifying, and incorporating new ideas. The skills needed will include communication skills, thinking skills, and perhaps a few technical skills.

The following questions are examples you might use to start your inquiry:

- What forces that support change are at work in the environment?
- How do I know it is time for a change?
- What will the change mean to me?
- Who will be affected by the change?
- What is their stake in the outcome?
- What will the change mean to them?
- Who will be willing and able to help bring the change to fruition?
- Who will oppose the change?
- Are there others who are already working toward the change I intend?
- Why hasn't this change already happened?
- Who should be at the table when decisions need to be made?
- What resources are already available?
- What additional resources will I need?
- Where will I do this? Do I need office space? Meeting space?
- Who will help legitimize the change?
- Are there organizations or agencies that need to be involved?
- How are decisions made in these organizations? In the community?
- How do local history and culture affect potential changes?
- What are the sources of diverse opinions?

- Are there methods or structures in place for finding common ground?
- Who are the recognized leaders?
- How is power distributed?
- What norms and standards do I need to be aware of?
- Are there compliance issues that I might face?
- What are the sources of data?
- Do I have access to all the information I need?
- How will I know when I have achieved what I set out to do?
- Who should be involved in evaluating the results?
- Is there a core group of people I can assemble for advice and guidance?

And you have probably already thought of several more questions which are pertinent to your situation. Essentially, the core questions to be addressed in the probing phase are What's going on? Who cares? and Why?

You must sharpen your awareness of the context. Immersion in the milieu will guide your decisions concerning changes you intend. Greenleaf (1991) captures this idea in his discussion of leadership perception:

> Framing all of this is awareness opening wide the doors of perception so as to enable one to get more of what is available of sensory experience and other signals from the environment than people usually take in. . . . When one is aware, there is more than usual alertness, more intense contact with the immediate situation, and more is stored away in the unconscious computer to produce intuitive insights in the future when needed. (p. 19)

The nature of the context for change informs leaders and followers while they engage in activity designed to change the nature of the context. A purposeful exploration of the day-to-day activity, relationships, values, deep beliefs, hopes and intentions that shape the context is the base upon which effective leaders build toward a better future. The process incorporates the theoretical perspective of situational leadership which holds that the situation determines and shapes the leader. However, it is my belief that the context helps us to find ways to share leadership and change the context. The discovery process is nonlinear, riddled with uncertainty, and designed to learn about an organic system rather than to reduce the situation to its smallest elements in order to discover its "truth."

SUMMARY

As your awareness of the context in which you intend to bring about changes develops, the vision you created in the previous chapter is sharpened. The work in Chapter 4 is intended to help you gain a clearer sense of your mission—your reason for leading. Determining what questions are important to your understanding of the context and then actively seeking answers, even as new questions are generated, involves incorporating multiple perspectives into your own thinking. As you do so, you will recognize the influence that your values and beliefs have on your vision and mission. As you will discover in the next chapter, their influence also becomes evident in your personal leadership philosophy.

REFLECTION, APPLICATION, AND RESOURCES

Questions for reflection and journaling:

1. How does your mission statement relate to your vision for change? Does it clearly move you in the direction needed?

2. What questions that aren't listed above are germane to your change situation? Why are they important?

Learning activities:

1. Do a personal preference assessment using the Personal Profile System or a similar tool. Get beyond finding your "label" and do the rest of the exercises in the booklet. Then, ask someone who knows you well to do the same assessment answering questions and making choices as they think you

would. Compare the results and reflect on the differences and similarities.

2. Draw a mind map of the context within which you intend to bring about change. Start with a central image in the middle of a very large piece of paper. Then, as you brainstorm key words to explore the context, use colors, codes, and symbols to generate a map to connect all the elements of the situation to the central image.

3. Search for the mission statements of organizations with whom you do business. They often appear in mailings, annual reports, or home pages on the World Wide Web. When you have several, compare them for content, clarity, and style. Does each one truly reflect what the organization does based on your experience?

Suggested readings and resources:

1. Personal Profile System booklets are available through Carlson Learning Company in Minneapolis, MN.

2. Snyder-Nepo's "Leadership Paper #4—Leadership Assessments: a Critique of Common Instruments" is available through the National Clearinghouse for Leadership Programs, University of Maryland, College Park. It provides a brief overview of dozens of assessment tools.

3. Covey's book, *Principle-Centered Leadership*, has a great deal to say about the importance of mission statements.

4. See Vaill's piece on "Contextuality" (pp. 122–125) in *Managing As a Performing Art*.

5. *Visionary Leadership*, by Burt Nanus has a wonderful chapter called "Considering the Possibilities: The Vision Context." See in particular his seven key questions on page 84.

CHAPTER 5

A Personal Philosophy of Leadership

As a returning adult student, I struggled with the perplexing process of rediscovering who I was and what I wanted to do with my life. I felt that some of the professors did not take into consideration that I had a life outside of classes. Granted, the circumstances that compelled me to go back to school, which I described in the first chapter, suggested that I had not been very successful. Still, I had experience in what was often referred to as the "real world." Although I valued book learning, I also believed that meaning comes from trying out ideas, applying concepts, and reflecting on experience. I was challenged to examine just who this "mature" person was and what that meant. One professor in particular served as both catalyst and guide for me in that process. The context for this self-assessment was the Philosophy of Adult Education class I mentioned previously.

The class was a turning point for me both personally and professionally. I have reflected on that process often in writing this book. It was a time of discovery, of getting to the core of me. I examined my assumptions, attitudes, beliefs, and values. I sorted through those I grew up with and considered the influence of my personal history. I decided which values and beliefs were really mine and discarded some that I had inherited which didn't seem to fit for me. I came to realize that my personal philosophy was very close to that of the person who led me to these discoveries. But, I also know that I didn't simply adopt his philosophy. My philosophy emanates from and grows within my own living, guiding, grounding source. The dilemma for me as I write, however, is to do justice to his influence and at the same time, claim what is mine because it is who I am.

A PHILOSOPHICAL FOUNDATION

Just as familiarity with leadership literature is not a substitute for leading, reading about leadership philosophy is not enough to provide a personal foundation for your own leadership. Developing a working philosophy draws upon what you learn from books and is deepened and personalized by your experience as well as your value orientation and belief system. Because leading is about creating change, the "starting point, as with all change, is to get clear within ourselves" (Block, 1993, p. 75). This chapter presents a process to guide you through that work.

The term working philosophy is descriptive for two reasons. In the first place, your philosophy continues to evolve over time, incorporating nuance and meaning derived from actually leading. Second, in conjunction with the fundamental beliefs and values you hold, your philosophy is contextually bound. This does not mean that you simply adopt a new philosophy for each new situation in which you find yourself. Instead, your philosophy relates to the context in which you are leading, suggesting unique leadership approaches while testing your assumptions and values in different situations.

A leadership philosophy is the personal lens through which we see how to behave as a leader. It emanates from the core and serves as the moral and ethical compass which gives direction to our actions. In discovering our personal philosophy, we find answers to three very basic questions (adapted from Apps, 1973).

1. What is real? (the metaphysical question) How does one distinguish between appearances and what actually is? For instance, the sun appears to orbit the earth, yet we know this is not the case.

2. How do we know? (the epistemological question) What is knowledge and what are the sources of knowledge? For example, when science cannot provide an answer to a question, where do we go for an explanation?

3. What is of value? (the axiological question) How does one decide what is right and what is wrong? What is good or bad? To illustrate, one may place high value on honesty but stop short of telling someone that his or her voice is very annoying to listen to for very long.

Answers to these basic questions form the foundation of your personal philosophy. In addition, as you reflect on the situation within which you are learning and leading, you can gain a sense of the philosophical orientation of other individuals as well as that of your organization or community. First you must do some deep personal searching. Once you clarify and claim your answers to these questions and others implied by them, it is very likely that you will be true to your own values and beliefs rather than succumb to the clamor of the times or the persuasiveness of others' positions on issues. You will see that your most basic assumptions, attitudes, values, and beliefs will hold true whatever the context. If you are to be authentic as a leader, you must live your philosophy all the time.

ASSUMPTIONS, ATTITUDES, VALUES, AND BELIEFS

In previous chapters, reference has been made to the need to go inside yourself to explore assumptions, attitudes, values, and beliefs about leadership. Taken together, they form the essence of your leadership philosophy. As we begin that discovery process, it is helpful to clarify the meaning of these terms to understand just what we will be probing for as we proceed.

Assumptions are those ideas which we take for granted and believe to be true. We build expectations based on the assumptions we make and take action based on our hypotheses. Generally, we don't challenge our assumptions, in part because we are often unaware that they exist even though they are manifested daily in what we do. Senge uses the term *mental models* and cites as an example, "At its heart, the traditional view of leadership is based on assumptions of people's powerlessness, their lack of personal vision and inability to master the forces of change, deficits which can be remedied only by a few great leaders" (1990, p. 340).

Attitudes describe the manner in which we think, act, or feel that reflects the opinions we hold. They are indicative of how we are disposed toward something or someone. We respond in predictable ways to evaluations we make concerning our likes and dislikes. An examination of our attitudes about ourselves, about our interactions with others, about the future, and about what we can intentionally accomplish to influence the future is essential to our understanding of how we will lead (Gardner, 1990; Hughes, Ginnett, & Curphy, 1993).

Values are qualitative estimates we make regarding worth. They are innate preferences we have with respect to principles and personal standards, methods of conduct, or desirable states of existence. Our value orientation gives rise to a whole set of likes and dislikes which are the building blocks of our moral and ethical foundation. One of the principles for clarifying values is that our values come through in how we communicate and are displayed in all our actions (Vaill, 1989, pp. 55–58).

Beliefs go beyond likes and dislikes to those ideas and tenets that we accept as true. We hold our beliefs as facts, confident of their reality. All that we believe forms the foundation for our convictions and is trusted implicitly. Green (1992), in writing about leadership in higher education, says that "our beliefs about leadership in American society and in higher education are grounded in a combination of common sense, intuition, and faith." Then she underscores what was said earlier in this chapter when she adds, "While there are numerous empirical studies of effective leadership in organizations, the literature is confusing and often contradictory" (p. 57).

Of primary concern in developing your working philosophy of leadership is identifying a set of core beliefs and values. As outlined by Apps (1994), there are several dimensions to core beliefs: reality and people (concerning the nature of human nature, of time, of organizations, and of the relationship of individuals to society and to the environment); knowledge (pertaining to how we know, sources of knowledge, intuition, wisdom, and truth); aesthetics (about art and beauty); and ethics (concerning justice, morality, and ethical decision making). He goes on to list examples of values to consider: "honesty, concern for family, commitment to children, integrity, being a citizen of the globe, justice, human rights, fairness, concern for nature and the physical environment, and faith in a spiritual being" (p. 80). As we turn our attention to exploring our personal leadership philosophy, we will add another layer of beliefs and values to those which we just described as fundamental. These are contextual beliefs and values, those bounded by a specific context, in this case leadership. Additionally, we may discover as we continue our introspection that we have some unconscious beliefs and values as well. These are beliefs and values that influence our thoughts and actions even though we may be unaware of them until they are somehow affronted. We simply take them for granted otherwise.

Let's turn now to some questions that can get you started examining your own values and beliefs within the context of leadership. The context, your values and beliefs, and a credo statement are the essential elements of your working philosophy of leadership.

QUESTIONS TO ASK

The questions below provide a starting place. They have evolved over time but can be traced back to the philosophy course I mentioned at the beginning of this chapter (Apps, 1973). As you read through them, you might want to start making a few notes. You may find other questions come to mind that you will want to jot down to stretch your thinking even further. Next, develop statements concerning your beliefs and values relative to each question. As you do so, consider the influence of assumptions you are making and attitudes you may have about leaders and leading. These questions are intended to provoke reflection and deep self-examination. The process will take time, so don't expect to get through them in a half hour!

To begin, let's focus on four sets of questions:

1. Beliefs and values about human nature:

   - The moral issue—is human nature essentially good or inherently evil?
   - What is the relationship between mind and body and spirit?
   - How do people interact in an organization?
   - How do people interact in a community?
   - Do people influence society or does society influence people?
   - Are humans a part of society or, to some degree, apart from society?
   - How much control over the natural world is appropriate?

2. Beliefs and values concerning the overall purpose of leadership:

   - To what extent is the purpose of leadership . . .
     . . . to provide people with resources which will help them make adjustments to their social conditions and natural world?
     . . . to provide people with resources to solve their own problems?
     . . . to protect people from what the future holds?
     . . . to help people change social conditions?
     . . . to help people become free, autonomous individuals?
     . . . to make good decisions for people?
     . . . to serve society in general?
     . . . to serve underrepresented populations?

3. Beliefs about what constitutes "leadership":

   - Is leadership of value by itself?
   - Is there something inherently good in leadership?

- Are there certain qualities that all leaders should have?
- What are the roles leadership plays?
- Is leadership only of value when it helps people to solve problems?
- How is leadership acquired?
- How should leadership be determined?
- Who decides who leads?
- What are sources of leader credibility?

4. Beliefs concerning the leadership process:

- Are organizational goals a guide for determining leadership action?
- Does leadership create vision or promote shared vision?
- Are leadership behaviors derived from personal experiences or developed externally?
- Should the quality of leadership always be evaluated in behavioral terms?
- Is the leadership development process . . .
    . . . training of the mind and acquisition of basic truths?
    . . . conditioning or reinforcement?
    . . . the development of insight?
    . . . experiential and reflective?
    . . . a lifelong learning process?

For each set of questions, think about the assumptions you make, your attitudes, the values you hold, and your core beliefs. Write down what comes to mind, including additional questions to consider. You might want to keep a separate journal for this work because it is likely that you will return to it occasionally as you continue to reflect on your leadership. Be introspective as you focus on how you lead and why, looking for the implications inherent in what you value and believe. Being who you are at the deepest level of your beliefs is being authentic. As pointed out earlier, your philosophy of leadership must be in harmony with your philosophy of life.

YOUR CREDO

As your sense of who you are as a leader emerges, it is time to write your credo. The word *credo* comes from Latin and means, literally, I believe. It is slightly different from a mission statement in that it is a personal statement of beliefs and principles. When you think through a personal credo statement and commit it to paper, it will serve as your touchstone for decisions and actions in any situation, "as a kind of personal guidance system for functioning . . . helping [you] live and work purposefully and decently in the midst of seeming paradox and contradiction" (Vaill, 1989, p. 212).

Apps (1994) suggests writing them as "I will . . . " statements because they take values and beliefs to the next level, expressing what you want to be and do as a leader. Arrange your statements in a way that has meaning for you. There are no rules for format or content. Here are a few examples to illustrate:

I will search for goodness in all the people with whom I work.
I will listen to my inner guides and act accordingly.
I will be open to multiple perspectives and incorporate new ideas in my thinking.
I will lead as I would like to be led.
I will balance my desire for success with the needs of others for involvement.
I will respect the right of others to disagree with me.
I will make time each day for reflection and introspection.

Your list will probably be much longer than this and may have very different language—as it should be since it will be uniquely yours.

Credo statements, once carefully derived and committed to paper, are not likely to change much because they are how you intend to manifest your innermost values and beliefs, and they are the deepest expression of your philosophy of leadership. As you lead and engage other people in creating changes that will result in a better future in which to live and work, these guiding principles will be tested. You will find conflicting values that are important to what you hope to be doing as a leader, in many relationships. It is important to be grounded in your credo

statement so that you are not unduly influenced by these conflicting values.

SUMMARY

I have said earlier that *Leading from Within* is not about
leadership but about YOU—being a leader, doing leadership.
Actions such as goal setting, conflict management, delegating
and the like are often thought of as the doing of leadership.
However, when you put yourself in the picture as the person
leading, there is an implied expectation that you will act in accord with your philosophy and with full understanding of the
context within which you are leading.

Being a leader means doing the inner work, using your
thinking skills and your innate intuitive ability to clearly articulate your reason for leading, create a vision, develop your mission, and immerse yourself in the context within which you intend to bring about changes. This takes us through to the first
blank in the framework for leading introduced in Chapter 1. In
the following chapter, we turn our attention to relationships,
the second blank in LEADERSHIP FOR _____ WITH
_____.

REFLECTION, APPLICATION, AND RESOURCES

Questions for reflection and journaling:

1. Are you aware of the assumptions that you make every day?
   For example, what are your underlying assumptions for a
   common activity like grocery shopping?

2. What attitudes might prove to be barriers to change? What
   attitudes might evoke change?

3. Which of your possessions do you value most? Why?

4. Are you superstitious? What do you believe about the relationship between superstition and fear?

5. Consider your working philosophy of leadership. How does it relate to the theories and definitions from the literature in Chapters 1 and 2?

Learning activities:

1. Reread the personal account at the beginning of this chapter. What observations might be made concerning the philosophy of the writer?

2. Conflict occurs when your philosophy is markedly different from those with whom you associate. Think about stories you read when you were young which might illustrate this. *Watership Down* by Richard Adams is one that comes to my mind. It tells of the struggles, romances, myths, and temptations of a community of rabbits. The context for the story is full of conflict based on differing philosophies among the rabbits and with the humans living nearby. Reread a story from your childhood and consider the philosophies of the various characters.

3. The symbols we use to denote leadership (for example, eagle, pyramid, raised fist, circle or web, tree) are grounded in our philosophy. Think about leadership symbols you have used and what they might be telling you about your philosophy. Ask people around you what their symbols are and then discuss yours with them, paying special attention to the values and beliefs expressed or implied.

4. The first Learning Activity in Chapter 1 asked you to design a leadership model. Reconfigure that model to incorporate what you have learned about your personal philosophy of leadership.

Suggested readings and resources:

1. A useful book for getting in touch with yourself is *I'm OK— You're OK* by T. A. Harris written in 1967.

2. *Values Leadership: Toward a New Philosophy of Leadership* by G. W. Fairholm offers an interesting perspective.

3. J. W. Apps's book, *Leadership for the Emerging Age* deals specifically with understanding your personal philosophy within the context of continuing education organizations. *Leadership by Design* by E. G. Bogue discusses philosophy in higher education institutions.

4. For a glimpse at Eastern mysticism, see Chapters 5 through 9 in Capra's *The Tao of Physics*. His connection between mysticism and physics is fascinating, particularly in light of new thinking about quantum organizations.

5. Vaill, in *Managing As a Performing Art*, presents ten principles of values clarification on pages 55–58. See also, page 212, for a brief discussion of Vaill's credo.

CHAPTER 6

Leaders, Stakeholders, and Followers

Several years ago, I was one of the leaders of a project called Partners in Natural Resource Policy (PNRP). It was one of a group of projects sponsored by the W. K. Kellogg Foundation that focused on coalition building and public policy education. Of the eleven projects funded, PNRP was playfully tagged the subversive program because of the emphasis placed on grass roots involvement. Ten of the project teams put together the coalition first and then led it through a policy education program. Ours went to the people first to find out what they perceived to be important natural resource policy issues and encouraged the formation of a coalition over time.

Our pilot effort was in Santa Cruz county, located in the southern part of Arizona and bordering Sonora, Mexico. More than four hundred interviews were conducted during which residents were asked what natural resource issues were important to them and the extent to which they felt they might have some influence in future policy decisions. Bilingual interviewers offered each respondent the choice of speaking Spanish or English during the interview process. We shared the findings broadly through local media and county government channels. Then, through a series of discussion meetings in small communities throughout the county, interested citizens decided to plan and implement an educational program to explore various alternatives and consequences of proposed policies concerning the natural resource issue of greatest interest, water availability and quality.

Meetings were called to bring the various stakeholders together: landowners along the dry Santa Cruz river bed, cattle ranchers, the National Park Service, local health officials from both sides of the border, Cooperative Extension Service educators, citizen groups, high school students, recreation enthusiasts, bird watchers, and so on. The varied perspectives made for lively debate, but the discussion soon focused on creating a way for all residents of the county to become more aware of the importance of managing the dry river bed and protecting the water interests for future generations. The planning galvanized around a series of events to be held over a period of several weeks which came to be called Discover the River or, in Spanish, *Descubra el Río*. At several key locations, the public was invited to "walk the river" with dozens of experts who would explain the geology, history, riparian habitat, water table, and cultural influences, and talk about other topics that affected water quality and availability.

The series culminated with a public forum held in the border city of Nogales. Here, ideas and opinions were expressed (in both Spanish and English with the help of simultaneous translators) and initial plans were made to continue the effort by creating a coalition to carry on the educational programs and work together to influence public policy. So, the story has no end. Even now, several years since the grant money ran out, a coalition which calls itself Friends of the Santa Cruz continues to do research and plan programs to educate and involve local citizens in policy discussions. In addition, a sister organization has formed in the neighboring county called Friends of the San Pedro, patterning its efforts after the successful model which evolved from the Partners project.

The story of the Partners project hints at the richness of the relationships among people with a stake in the future of the Santa Cruz River. The context for change in this instance was influenced by the uniqueness of the Arizona/Sonora border culture. Probing the context is an ongoing effort which helps us to understand the people who will be sharing responsibility for creating a better future in which to live and work. We turn our attention now to the leadership relationship and the ways people come together to bring about intended changes.

LEADERSHIP AS A RELATIONSHIP

In the second chapter, an overview of some of the historical definitions of leadership was presented along with a brief discussion of the broad contextual elements which are influencing the meaning of leadership as the twentieth century draws to a close. At this point in time, there is general agreement that leadership is a relationship rather than simply a list of traits or a series of behaviors. The leadership relationship encompasses leaders, followers, stakeholders, and the context. A glimpse of the more current definitions of leadership reflects this perspective:

- "Leadership is a relationship between leaders and followers" (Kouzes & Posner, 1987, p. 1).
- "Leadership is a reciprocal relationship between those who choose to lead and those who decide to follow" (Kouzes & Posner, 1993, p. 1).
- "Leadership is an influence relationship among leaders and followers who intend real changes that reflect their mutual purposes" (Rost, 1991, p. 102).
- "Leadership is the articulation of new values and the energetic presentation of them to those whose actions are affected by them" Vaill (1989, p. 55).
- "The successful leader is also a good follower, one who is committed to ideas, values and beliefs" (Sergiovanni, 1990, p. 23).
- "Leadership is not what the leader does, but what leaders and collaborators do together" (Earnest, 1994, p. 1).
- "Leadership does not occur without followers, and good leaders are also good followers" (Hughes, Ginnett, & Curphy, 1993, p. 19).

It seems clear, then, that much of the work of the leader is to develop relationships which are important to the changes intended.

When we begin to see ourselves leading, we may feel as if we are all alone. However, it is rare that the change we envision does not involve others. To the best of my knowledge, change always involves others, some actively and some indifferently, perhaps even unknowingly. Some may be supporters, some may be resistors, some may be legitimizers, and some may be neutral initially but with the potential to either support or resist the change effort.

Understanding how others affect the changes we intend is best undertaken with an attitude of openness and inclusiveness. Trying to control change through excluding others will not work. It is unfortunate if those who can be of valuable assistance are not part of the interchange of ideas. Even those who may seem uninterested or who are outwardly opposed may have a great deal to contribute. We won't know unless we develop a relationship with them.

STAKEHOLDERS

Individuals who have a stake in the change process or its outcomes need to be involved to the extent feasible. Sometimes identifying the stakeholders is a daunting task because we might not know all those who will either be affected by or have the ability to influence the intended change. We start with the most obvious stakeholders and then examine the ripple effect. In the Partners project story related at the beginning of this chapter, the list of stakeholders grew over time as familiarity with the context deepened. A number of them are listed in the story. As anticipated, each group of stakeholders came into the story with its own happy ending in mind. The challenge was to provide the opportunity for all participants to include their points of view and then look for the common ground.

In any situation where diverse perspectives are present, conflicts may arise among stakeholders whose values, beliefs, and goals differ from ours and from each other's. For example, not all stakeholders will have the same degree of interest in bringing about the changes we have in mind, and some may be adamantly opposed. There is likely to be disagreement concerning the perceived benefits and relative costs to the various stakeholders. Conflicts are to be expected and the ensuing debates could be acrimonious. However, if we can get beyond debate and discussion, open dialogue can breed innovative ideas and create new meaning. Successful dialogue is a powerful communication tool incorporating new ways of thinking and producing surprising and satisfying results. Unlike debate, there are no winners and losers in dialogue. When we debate, the intent is to win an argument. When we discuss, it is to consider an issue. When we engage in dialogue, our purpose is to generate new ideas and understanding. This is the ultimate goal of any relationship.

Often, the relationships we develop in exploring context grow out of our need to connect within our own organization or to establish linkages with other organizations and institutions. An entire organization can offer support, resistance, legitimation, or be neutral just as individuals can. We need to find out about norms, structures, decision-making processes and philosophy, to consider the diverse viewpoints, and to determine their potential relationship to the intended changes. Whether we are dealing with individuals or organizations, multiple perspectives are characteristic of the relationships with stakeholders in any change context.

FOLLOWERS

The more recent leadership definitions cited earlier in this chapter make it clear that followers are essential players in the leadership relationship. Understanding that relationship will "unravel the many layers of meaning of any given problem or solution" (Green, 1992, p. 61). In this way, leaders and followers "develop mutual purposes" (Rost, 1991, p. 122) rather than relate simply as supervisor telling subordinate what to do. Rost goes on to explain what developing mutual purposes means:

> The changes that leaders and followers intend must reflect their mutual purposes. Mutual purposes are common purposes, not only because

they are forged from the influence relationship, which is inherently non-coercive, not only because they develop over time from the multi-directional nature of the relationship, *but because the followers and leaders together do leadership* [italics in the original]. Leadership is their common enterprise, the essence of the relationship, the process by which they exert influence. (p. 122)

Development of mutual purposes may not happen readily without some motivating spark. The will to explore and act is sometimes inherent in an unstable situation but, more often than not, part of the leader's role is to motivate followers. To do so effectively calls on the whole self to know how to express hope, ignite the quest for justice, kindle a hunger to understand things, and to share the experience of awe, wonder and reverence (Gardner, 1990).

Leaders need to know when to step out of the leadership role and become followers. Effective leaders are also followers; effective followers are also leaders. This exchange of roles and the interplay that results are what make for shared leadership, the hallmark of commitment and high performance. This is often referred to as teamwork. Personally, I avoid using the word "team" because it reflects an old paradigm that I don't believe captures the essence of the relationship. It is a sports metaphor grounded in winning as the desired result and in the need for individuals to carry out a specific role or function in order to be successful. The leader in this configuration is the coach and the team depends on his or her direction. For me, shared leadership means shared power and a sense of interdependence more like that found in community than on a team. Notice how we talk about "in" community and "on" a team. The team is externally conceived and the community is an organism of which we are an integral part.

EFFECTIVE FOLLOWERS, EFFECTIVE LEADERS

What characterizes effective followership? We must let go of the imagery of shepherds and docile sheep, the pied piper and rats, or the officer and blindly obedient soldiers to understand followers in the relationship we're trying to build to bring about change. In his thought-provoking book, Kelley (1992) claims "followership and leadership are a dialectic. Just as the word 'right' makes no sense without 'left,' they depend on each other for existence and meaning. They can never be independent" (p. 45). Followers, while in the act of following, are likely to be leading at the same time. Kelley (1992) goes on to describe what it is that effective followers do. They add value to the situation through focus and commitment, competence in task activities, and personal initiative to increase their value to the organization or community. They nurture and leverage relationships with team members, organizational or community networks, and leaders. And they exercise a courageous conscience on the job and in relationships. Their courage to speak out, connection with other stakeholders and contributors, independent thinking and problem solving ability may be the key to a successful effort. Just as leaders do not lead all the time, neither do followers follow all the time. In large measure, the exchange of roles is bounded by the nature of the relationship and the reason for coming together.

What characterizes effectiveness in the leadership relationship? Hughes, Ginnett and Curphy (1993) claim that good leadership makes a difference but what constitutes good leadership is neither simple nor constant. They see effectiveness as a function of the relationship of the leader, the followers, and the situation. It varies with the context. McCall (1993) reports that studies point to six basic characteristics of effective leadership: (1) an ability to translate direction and mission into reality, (2) an ability to align people with the chosen direction, (3) integrity and the ability to develop trust, (4) comfort with uncertainty, (5) strong self-awareness, and (6) constant learning and adaptation. Kouzes and Posner (1987) cite five practices exhibited by successful leaders: (1) they challenge the process, (2) inspire a shared vision, (3) enable others to act, (4) model the way, and (5) encourage the heart. Apps (1994) says that effective leaders for the emerging age are those who create and communicate a vision, build bridges between people and ideas, embrace ambiguity, applaud serendipity, encourage artistry, tolerate and even encourage discomfort, reflect on activities, appreciate humor, take risks, and challenge ideas, structures, assumptions, and beliefs. From my perspective, being an effective leader may mean being able to do all these things. However, it is more likely that others who are involved in the leader/follower relationship have some of these talents and can be relied upon to exchange roles when needed.

In the 1970s, Burns's (1978) view was that leadership was only effective when changes were realized which met people's enduring needs. In the 1990s, Rost (1991) takes an entirely different stance. He claims that "effectiveness or whatever synonym is used—achievement, results, excellence, products, success, peak performance—is not an essential element of leadership" (p. 116). From his perspective, the intent to bring about changes undergirds the leadership relationship regardless of whether those changes are actually achieved. Just as the definitions of leadership have been modified over time, so too have notions of what constitutes effective leadership. For our purposes, effectiveness is defined within the context. It is determined primarily by those involved in the leadership relationship and the circumstances that bring them together. For example, effective leaders in the Partners Project were those who could maintain credibility as experts (as an economist, range management specialist, geologist, and the like) while they actively sought to find common ground among the disparate interests and create new understanding of the complexity of the river ecology. Those who simply stood their ground and tried to convince others that there was only one "right" point of view were not as effective in this particular situation.

WAYS PEOPLE COME TOGETHER

Sometimes the relationship involves just two people at a time, but very often the leadership relationship involves groups of people. How we interact with people is influenced by the manner which brings us together to get something done. Several examples of ways people relate to each other are given below. You may note that each one of them begins with "com-" or its variation "co-," prefixes derived from the Latin word for "with" which for our purposes means together, jointly, or mutually. Each of the relationships is described in terms of what is shared.

When we come together to *communicate*, we **share information** through the expression of thoughts, questions, ideas, and opinions. The expression may involve spoken language, written words, and even body language. Stories are told, messages are passed along, wisdom is imparted, and information is made known.

A *committee* comes together to discuss policy, hear reports, and assign tasks that are part of a **shared agenda**. Development of the agenda may take place outside of the committee and then be presented. Often, one or more committee members will have responsibility for deciding the topics and flow of an agenda, particularly if there are subcommittees with reports to file. Committees are generally chosen to reflect a single view in support of a matter to be considered. They have an assigned charge and are expected to report or act on some matter.

When people decide to *cooperate* they maintain their independent perspective but agree to **shared action** to produce an effect or achieve mutual benefits. Acting together produces a greater effect. It is a way to achieve a common objective even though the long-term goals may be quite different. Sometimes, however, cooperation may simply mean an agreement of noninterference. Generally, people are motivated to cooperate because it is a way to have more influence than any of them can muster individually.

Collaboration is a process that occurs when people **share the responsibility** involved in a joint endeavor. It has been described as the constructive management of differences, a particularly apt expression when applied to, for example, collaboration in the arts or literature (Gray, 1989). Working together with an agreed goal in mind, people take advantage of the strengths and minimize the shortcomings of those engaged in the collaboration.

Members of a *coalition* **share power** even though they may not share the same philosophy. When disparate views are superseded by a higher cause, the commitment to a course of action with long-term benefits results in interdependence and a redistribution of power. Often, a temporary alliance is formed when several factions come together in times of emergency, pitting their combined strength against the perceived threat. As an example, at the beginning of this chapter I described how the Friends of the Santa Cruz formed around the threat of a diminishing water supply that was potentially unhealthy.

In *community* people have a **shared future** that emanates from a collective vision of their common destiny. Traditionally, community is thought of in terms of a particular place where a person lives and has close personal associations. Recently, we have begun to discover ways to create community in the workplace. From my perspective, community can exist whenever or wherever people are drawn together over common interest and a shared vision of the future.

At different times, each of these ways of coming together for the purpose of sharing is the most appropriate way to relate to one another. In my opinion however, the reason for leading has to do with community. As Matusak (1997) points out, "Once people experience the spirit of community, they have . . . a desire to achieve it again. This collective spirit, this interdependence of independent people needs to be nurtured" (p. 71).

SUMMARY

In this chapter, we have looked at the nature of the leadership relationship. The number of people who have a stake in the changes you intend to bring about may surprise you. However, not all stakeholders will choose to be part of the change process, to become followers. For those who do become involved, examples of the characteristics of effective followers have been presented. Similarly, effectiveness of leaders in the leadership relationship has been briefly discussed. The chapter ends with a brief description of different ways people come together around their shared goals. This sets the stage for the discussion in Chapter 7 on building community.

REFLECTION, APPLICATION, AND RESOURCES

Questions for reflection and journaling:

1. What does it mean to be a good follower? Are you a good follower? Why?

2. The Great Law of the Iroquois Confederacy includes this assertion: In all our deliberations, we must consider the impact on the next seven generations. What does this mean concerning possible stakeholders within the context of natural resource issues and policy decisions?

3. Gardner (1990, p. 199) says: "In the conventional mode people want to know whether the followers believe in the leader; a more searching question is whether the leader believes in the followers." Reflect on your personal experience and write about what this means to you.

Learning activities:

1. Legos or Tinker Toys are excellent for this activity. Or, if they are not available, just gather some office supplies and desk items to use as building material. Reflect for a moment on your context for change. Then, build a model representing the various stakeholders involved, their relationship to each other, and their connection with you and the change you envision. Study your model a bit and then explain it to a friend or co-worker. Their perspective may generate questions to help you clarify various aspects of your model.

2. Keep track of your interactions with people around you (at work, in school, at home) for a day or two. Think about the nature of your interactions and the type of association you have in each situation. Reflect on whether they involve de-

bate, discussion or dialogue. List interactions by type: communication, committee, cooperation, collaboration, coalition, community. Which one(s) felt productive to you? Why?

Suggested readings and resources:

1. Robert Kelley's book, *The Power of Followership*, broke new ground by challenging us to consider "followership" as not only a worthy endeavor, but as the source of self-leadership. It contains information about followership styles and skills of effective followers.

2. In Chaleff's *The Courageous Follower: Standing Up To and For Our Leaders* a model of followership is presented which assures us that following need not be passive.

3. Within the context of community education programs, Miller, Rossing, and Steele examine three themes: empowering stakeholders, developing and maintaining partnerships, and leadership among and by partners. See *Partnerships: Shared Leadership Among Stakeholders*.

4. More on stakeholders, including guidelines for a Stakeholder Assessment Process, may be found in Bryson and Crosby's book, *Leadership for the Common Good: Tackling Public Problems in a Shared-Power World*.

5. The Ohio Center for Action on Coalition Development for Families and High Risk Youth, under the direction of Richard Clark, has published a series of bulletins called *Building Coalitions* which is straightforward and contains a great deal of practical information.

CHAPTER 7

Building Community

Recently, when I asked a group of students to define a project to work on for the semester, they determined that they wanted to do something about improving communication on campus. Over the course of several weeks, they explored their context and eventually came to realize that what they were describing was a sense of their longing for a feeling of campus community. Some students were less than enthusiastic about this for a leadership project because they didn't see why or how it might effect them personally. However, we pressed forward and looked at a range of alternatives for initiating changes that might build campus connections and reduce the traditional polarities—students versus the "system," faculty versus administration, staff versus the reorganization of human resources, discipline versus discipline, teaching versus research, and so on.

Within the class, there were those who wanted to confront "them" and tell "them" what was wrong, and others who wanted to find out more about how members of the campus community viewed the situation before taking a stand. The discussion vacillated between anger at the various factions and hopelessness because so little was known about how things really worked on campus. Ultimately, the students decided that the key was in coming to an understanding about what community meant to various groups of stakeholders across campus. So, rather then telling people what was wrong from individual personal perspectives, and instead of continuing to study the situation to try to deduce a course of action, the students began to explore hosting and facilitating a campus forum to engage stakeholders in a dialogue about community on campus.

Using concepts and techniques learned in class, the students designed a process that they would facilitate for creating shared meaning about community on campus. It included a brief presentation of the context for the discussion which was followed by small group dialogue about the meaning of community. With that as background, the entire group was asked to reflect on a vision for what campus community might be like in the year 2020. The closing activity called for those present to decide what they might do, individually as well as collectively, to bring the vision to fruition. The participant guest list developed by the students included, among others, selected students, the university president, several from higher administration, a dean, a number of faculty, student advisors, staff from several units, people from campus communication and technology areas, representatives from human resources, and several from student services.

As the semester came to a close, we reflected on both the process and the outcomes of the forum. They learned first hand that community is not created by one person. They learned that community is a shared commitment that builds on stakeholders' expectations and actions. They learned that communication and reflection concerning a collective belief in a future desired state, one that both incorporates and transcends individual desires and values, is essential. They also learned that, in order to be effective leaders in helping build a sense of community on campus, they first had to build community within the context of the class project.

The class realized that outcomes of the campus community forum may not all be measurable in the classic sense of results-oriented educational programs. The extent of the impact of the forum was not even apparent. However, they came away with a clear sense that they had, for a moment, touched on something of value with people who recognized their own longing for community. It was an exercise of the heart. Those who had participated had willingly said, "I/we will do these things to contribute to building community on campus." The students knew that they had been leaders, acting as catalysts for positive changes to deepen the experience of community on campus.

The students' story illustrates that community is more than place. In this chapter, we will explore the meaning of community and describe different ways people experience community. A look at the stages of community formation will help us to better understand how they develop and how that influences the leadership relationship.

THE MEANING IN COMMUNITY

There are definitions of community and there is the experience of community. It is your personal experience that will give meaning to the definitions. Galbraith (1992) for example, talks of megacommunity which includes global as well as local manifestations. He defines megacommunity as "a large scale systematic community that is connected by cultural, social, psychological, economic, political, environmental, and technological elements" (p. 8). In his discussion, he cites current literature to characterize communities of place, communities of interest, and communities of function. Additionally, he suggests typing communities either demographically, using the black community as an example, or psychographically around value systems and lifestyle, citing the yuppy community to illustrate.

We experience community in a variety of ways, in a range of settings. Perhaps most typically, when we think of community, we think of a place—where we live, our neighborhood, where we grew up, where we went to school. More recently, the notion of community as a common place that we share with others is being applied to organizations where people work. Leaders, stakeholders, and followers are exploring the meaning of community and working together to create a sense of belonging to a community within the workplace. Flora, Flora, Spears, Swanson, Lapping, and Weinberg (1992) suggest that mobility and technology have also had an influence on how we experience community. Increasingly, a sense of community comes from those who do similar things or share common values, not from those living in the same town.

The key to community is found in the root of the word.

Community is a derivative of the Latin word *communitas* which means community or fellowship. *Communitas* comes from the word *communis* which means common. Although community gets its meaning from what people have in common when they come together, diversity is also present, flavoring and enriching community. A former student shared a summary of the world that serves to illustrate the presence of diversity in the global community. If we were to shrink the earth's population as it is now to a village of one hundred people, it would look like this:

- There would be 57 Asians, 21 Europeans, 14 from the Western Hemisphere and 8 Africans
- 70 would be nonwhite and 30 would be white
- 70 would be non-Christian and 30 would be Christian
- 50% of the entire world wealth would be in the hands of 6 people
- All 6 would be citizens of the United States
- 70 would be unable to read
- 50 would suffer from malnutrition
- 80 would live in substandard housing
- Only 1 would have a college education

And the list could go on to include other differences. Obviously, this list was developed by someone with a set of assumptions concerning which characteristics represented diversity, but there are many more.

The fact is, we live in a very diverse world. When we consider the range of differing values and beliefs in nearly every situation we find ourselves, we expand the idea of diversity well beyond race, creed, and color. There is a certain amount of comfort in associating with others very like ourselves. However, we grow and change when challenged by new ideas and different ways of thinking about what we do, what we feel, and what we believe. As we incorporate multiple perspectives into our own thought processes, we still maintain a sense of self and may even reach greater clarity regarding just who we are. Therein lies the beauty of diversity—we have our own identity while contributing to and believing in the whole community.

The essence of community is "a shared experience of belonging and contributing to something larger than oneself" (Campbell, 1995, p. 189). Community is not necessarily an automatic outcome when people come together around common goals and ideas. It derives from meaningful interaction with others. A healthy, vibrant community has a collective spirit that comes only with commitment to a shared destiny. It may begin as a tiny spark which must be fueled with caring concern for others, inclusion of diverse perspectives, and willingness to put the larger goal ahead of personal gain. The resulting flame then becomes the center around which people gather in a circle to be nourished, sustained, and enlightened.

Consider the community within which you intend to bring about change. What is the larger goal? Being a leader means developing a community of believers around mutual purposes. What is the nature of your community?

CLASSIC COMMUNITY DEVELOPMENT

Your context for change may be embedded in the community where you live, work, go to school, attend church, and get together with friends. Perhaps you have in mind to change a local ordinance or develop environmental policy. In many small communities throughout the country, local economic development is a catalyst for community involvement and action. Moore and Brooks (1996) describe what they call a different approach to community economic development. It is cited here because the processes suggested are similar to those employed in classic community development. They believe the differences inherent in the model are summarized in how a community does these four things:

1. Develops broad based *support* from residents throughout the community;

2. Creates a *shared vision* of what community change is and the individual's part of that vision;

3. Establishes a *climate for individual and group learning* from each other and about the community; and

4. Promotes a *willingness to work together* across political, social, racial, and economic boundaries. (p. 152)

The leadership function is easily shared in the setting described above as individuals with particular interests and/or expertise come forward throughout the process. Looking specifically at rural communities, Borich and Foley (1990) are quite clear in proclaiming that leadership "does not necessarily mean a single individual directing actions in a single municipality . . . Leadership is fluid in the context of place and numbers of people involved" (p. 110). Being a leader in a community of place means sharing the responsibility of working toward the common good.

COMMUNITY IN THE WORKPLACE

Your context for change may be within the organization where you work. Maynard and Mehrtens (1993) have written about what business in the next century might be like. It is their view that when organizational barriers between people are eliminated, "people become bonded, sensing that they can rely on and trust each other. When people achieve this feeling of community, their subsequent achievements are nothing short of miraculous" (p. 13). The changes you intend where you work are more likely to be successful if you invest time and energy in creating this sense of community. Autry (1991) describes the ideal community in the workplace in terms of the inherent implications:

> By invoking the metaphor of community, we imply that we in business are bound by a fellowship of endeavor in which we commit to mutual goals, in which we contribute to the best of our abilities, in which each contribution is recognized and credited, in which there is a forum for all voices to be heard, in which our success contributes to the success of the common enterprise and to the success of others, in which we can disagree and hold differing viewpoints without withdrawing from the

community, in which we are free to express what we feel as well as what we think, in which our value to society is directly related to the quality of our commitment and effort, and in which we take care of one another. (p. 80)

A commitment to common goals is grounded in the organization's vision and mission statement. If the place where you work doesn't have these, you will need to begin by bringing people together to create them. Or, if the vision and mission statement were created by the highest level in a hierarchy and are framed and hanging on the wall, you may need to determine if everyone agrees and feels ownership for this key element of the context. If not, ask yourself how you might bring people together to review and find meaning in the vision and mission, perhaps even revise the language to clarify the intent. If key decision makers are not willing to engage employees in discussion and scrutiny of their organizational vision and mission, you might be able to get them to legitimize a process whereby your workgroup could create its own and demonstrate linkages to the larger organization. In any case, commitment to the common enterprise goes hand in hand with meaningful work. The rest of Autry's metaphor emanates from a clear sense of why people are bound together in the endeavor. Creative problem solving and the shared leadership for achieving organizational goals are not likely to occur in an environment where the spirit of community is not nurtured. Being a leader in a workplace community means sharing the responsibility for carrying out the corporate mission. Paradoxically, it may also mean challenging both the mission and the vision.

BUILDING A COMMUNITY OF INTEREST

Your context for change may develop around an idea, a philosophical concern, or a societal issue about which you are passionate. As you recognize in others a kinship for your passion and then reach out to them with respect for their diverse viewpoints, the seed of community is planted. "Commitment to community is not unrelated to the problem of finding meaning

in life—an ancient problem but never more widespread than today" (Gardner, 1990, p. 189). Many citizen action groups begin
in just this way, searching for meaning in tragedy or injustice.
Noted anthropologist Margaret Meade has often been quoted
as saying, never doubt that a small group of thoughtful, committed citizens can change the world—indeed, it is the only
thing that ever has.

Ostendorf and Levitas (1987) describe the process aptly as
individuals moving from "a perspective of purely personal crisis
to one of community response—from 'coping' to 'poking'—
from mere adaptation to changing" (p. 62). As in the two types
of communities described earlier in this chapter, galvanizing
citizens around a social issue begins with the building of a clear
sense of purpose, a vision and mission which evolves from meaningful dialogue. Once again, there may not be total agreement
on ideology and methodology for moving in the direction of the
vision. When people working together see a higher purpose,
they can and will collaborate to effect positive change if the
spirit of community is nurtured. Being a leader and sharing the
responsibility for moving a community of believers to action
means understanding and applying the principles associated
with building, experiencing, and sustaining community.

ACHIEVING COMMUNITY

Whether you are dealing with a small group of people, a
neighborhood, a large city, or a complex organization, the path
to community is likely to be bumpy and to take occasional unexpected turns. An emerging community goes through several
phases before it reaches maturity. Gozdz (1995a, p. 10) describes
four stages in community building which generally correspond
to the four stages of group development—forming, storming,
norming, and performing—articulated by Parker (1990). The
group of students mentioned in the story at the beginning of
this chapter typifies this developmental process.

The early *forming* phase is called pseudo-community by
Gozdz and is characterized by polite behavior, dependence on

decisions made by others or by someone in charge, and differences go unchallenged or are ignored. For example, the students mentioned above waited for instructions as to what should be done, in what order, and by when. They were relatively quiet in class, and many were reluctant to speak openly about their own perspectives regarding the work to be done to complete their project.

Storming is the second stage, what Gozdz refers to as chaos. During this phase, differences become apparent, conflicts erupt, and emotions run high. People see issues in terms of polarities, spawning competition and resulting in winners and losers. In the classroom setting, students were critical of each other's ideas concerning the nature of the forum and who should be invited to participate. One person went so far as to declare that he wasn't going to invite anyone to come unless he could be sure that the process met his expectations.

Once differences are out in the open, the *norming* stage can begin. Gozdz calls this emptiness. Individual attempts to control the situation have been unsuccessful and people are feeling insecure and uncertain. Group cohesiveness overcomes competition as individuals begin to be more reflective, examining their stake in the effort, expressing their values and beliefs, and really listening to the diverse perspectives of those around them. It becomes possible for collaboration and group decision making to occur. The student project seemed in disarray and time was running out. Frustration gave way to dismay and some began to wonder if the project was doomed to fail. We used a personal assessment tool as a means to understand how individual preferences and ways of approaching the project might either be hindering or enhancing their progress in planning the forum. They began to listen to each other and to look for ways to capitalize on each person's strengths. Understanding grew from the dialogue and they began to make decisions collaboratively.

Gozdz' fourth stage is called community and corresponds to the *performing* phase of group activity. Authenticity in communication, acknowledgment of differences and willingness to commit to the larger goal are present in this stage. Individuals no longer feel threatened and so are freed up to be innovative and to risk self-disclosure. In the case of my students, the turning point came with the stark realization that in two weeks' time, three dozen people, including the president of the university, would sit down with the class to discuss the meaning of community. They recognized the need to commit to a collaborative effort not only because they didn't want to embarrass themselves, but because they understood that for the forum to be successful, they had to give up the need to try to control the process. Harmony developed as interdependence replaced competition. As the night of the campus community forum approached, the students were in frequent communication, the energy level was high, and expectations soared. They were ready to perform because they trusted each other.

These stages of community building should not be thought of as a discrete and linear process. Rather, they serve as a guide for what to expect in the early stages of community. In reality, creating and nurturing community is a cyclic process because the very nature of community is that of a dynamic organism, the attributes of which include an "emphasis on human interactions and relationships within places, and commonalities in interests, values, and mores" (Galbraith, 1992, p. 9). However simple or complex the community, as it matures, people are better able to sustain a high level of interdependence and forward momentum toward a shared destiny.

SUMMARY

Community means something personal to each of us that shapes and colors many definitions of the term. For me, as I suggested in an early chapter, management is related to teamwork while leadership is concerned with community. Community can encompass a particular location, an organization, an institution, an ideology, a lifestyle—some common denominator which brings people together in meaningful relationships and the desire for a shared future. Three types of community (place, work, and interest) were presented in this chapter as examples of what you might experience in your context for change. In addition, four stages of community building describe what you might expect to encounter. What leaders and followers do in each stage was illustrated through the story from the beginning of Chapter 7. The skills needed to be effective in building community vary depending on the stage and, to some extent, on the type of community in which you are involved. In the next chapter, a framework for developing a personal leadership education program is presented as a guide to developing the skills you will need in all aspects of your role as leader.

REFLECTION, APPLICATION, AND RESOURCES

Questions for reflection and journaling:

1. Think about community and context. How are they alike? How are they different?

2. Reflect on the context you began to explore in Chapter 4. Is your context already a community? Does it involve several communities? Do you see yourself building a new community around your issue or the changes you intend?

3. Consider some of the conflicts which may be inherent in your context. What do you know about the diversity these conflicts represent? What are some ways that you can incorporate differing perspectives? In what instances will you need to accommodate other values and beliefs? How will this influence the changes you intend?

Learning activities:

1. Look at the list early in this chapter which summarizes the earth's population in a village of one hundred people. Look for other statistics which you might incorporate to reflect other perspectives. For example, how many of the hundred would be teachers, writers, parents, under the age of three, living in cities, physically handicapped, and so on. Base your search on characteristics of interest to you.

2. In the story at the beginning of this chapter, the campus
   community served as the context for student learning. Silien,
   Lucas, and Wells (1992) offer the following definition of
   community as it applies to student learning on campus:
   "Community is the binding together of diverse individuals
   committed to a just, common good through shared experience in a spirit of caring and social responsibility" (p. 35).
   As you are learning and leading, does this definition fit the
   community where you live, work or go to school? Ask other
   stakeholders for their definition of community, compare, and
   use this as basis for discussion.

3. Generate a list of metaphors that you have heard used to describe or explain diversity. Which of these metaphors work
   well for you and which ones don't? For example, is diversity
   like a melting pot or a salad? Why? Then be creative and add
   new metaphors to the list that describe how you think of
   diversity.

Suggested readings and resources:

1. Drath and Palus have written a piece for the Center for Creative Leadership called "Making Common Sense: Leadership
   as Meaning-Making in a Community of Practice" which is
   excellent.

2. Senge has written a chapter called "Creating Quality Communities" in *Community Building* edited by Kazimierz Gozdz.
   It contains a wonderful discussion of learning organizations
   grounded in the development of leadership communities.

3. In *Training and Development* (May 1995), see Jill Janov's
   piece titled "Creating Meaning: The Heart of Learning Communities."

4. Two recommendations from *The Systems Thinker*: In volume
   5, number 7, look for an article by Greg Zlevor, "Creating
   a New Workplace: Making a Commitment to Community."
   His notion of a community/disciety [*sic*, Zlevor's invented
   word] continuum is quite intriguing. Also, in volume 6,

number 2, an article by Gozdz, "Building a Core Competence in Community," describes four main leadership skills
he sees as necessary for the task.

5. Manning, Curtis, and McMillen, in *Building Community:
   The Human Side of Work*, have a particularly good section
   on valuing human diversity. Their book also has a number
   of useful exercises to use as community building tools.

CHAPTER 8

Leading and Lifelong Learning

Recently, I was involved in the design and implementation of a leadership education program for department heads on our campus. An outgrowth of the continuous organizational renewal efforts championed by our president, the series of seminars was called the President's Quality Leadership Program (PQLP). My interest in facilitating a program designed to engage department heads in the transformation of the university was underscored by a growing sense that they longed for a means by which they might metaphorically sit in a circle and, face-to-face with their faculty, work collaboratively on complex problems.

There are many truly excellent scholars at our university serving in administrative roles. They are well recognized in their fields for their research efforts and their excellence in teaching. Many heads of departments were pressed into service based primarily on their reputation within their discipline. However, the skills needed for excellence in an academic discipline are not necessarily the same ones needed to provide leadership within a college or at the unit level. Whereas most academic units are well able to clarify what distinguishes them from any other discipline, and most faculty develop a line of scholarship uniquely theirs, leadership is a more integrative endeavor. Disciplinary reputations are built on specialization and competition among peers while leadership demands a more collaborative approach.

Among department heads, the role is generally an entry level leadership position. Many new heads come into the position without much investment in leadership education as part of their continuing professional development. Management skills which they honed on outstanding scholarship and/or exemplary

teaching need to be expanded to encompass leadership concepts
and approaches that are required to guide and support an academic unit. This is particularly true within the context of tur-
bulent times in higher education, an era in which many colleges
and universities are dealing with a seeming paradox: the need
to survive AND the need for transformation.

Some department heads were looking for the right answers,
some were looking for the right questions. A series of management mini-programs had been offered the previous semester for
those who were looking for information about current policy
and procedures. However, for those who were seeking better
questions and shared solutions, an alternative was needed. The
vision for PQLP was that transformational leadership would be
valued and supported throughout the university as the means
by which we would become recognized as both an outstanding
Land-Grant institution and a student-centered research university. The mission of PQLP was to enhance current and future
leadership capacity throughout the organization. Because department heads were viewed as critical players in the transformation of the university, the program goal was to engage them
in leadership development activities designed to increase their
conceptual understanding of leadership, provide opportunity
for practice and application of leadership concepts, and foster continued collaboration and communication linkages. Four
themes provided the framework for the seminar series:

1. Department Dynamics—The Systems Perspective

2. Leadership Effectiveness—The Personal Perspective

3. Building a Community of Excellence—The People
   Perspective

4. Leadership in Context—The Action Perspective

The department heads reported in the preliminary evalua-
tion that they were appreciative of the time spent together working within their own group to raise issues, discuss them, and
think about approaches to solutions. A number of them cited
specific applications of new ideas and use of the materials fol-

lowing the sessions. Perhaps the single most beneficial aspect of the program was reported to be the opportunity to connect with each other, to think and dream together, and to begin to develop a community of department heads. (Excerpts from Huber, 1996)

CONTINUOUS LEARNING

The story of PQLP serves as a capsule study illustrating how even well-educated leaders recognize the need for continued learning. Leaders have both the ability and the responsibility to take charge of their own learning. Leading and lifelong learning go hand in hand (Apps, 1994; Galbraith, 1992; Gardner, 1990; Senge, 1990; Vaill, 1996). Occasionally, this means returning to a classroom setting, but more often, learning takes place within the context in which we find ourselves. "Continuous learning is shaped by the way the situation is framed and by the capacity of individuals for the work they undertake" (Watkins & Marsick, 1993, pp. 32–33). As we learn from experience, we change, thus generating more learning opportunities. Learning while leading is transformational, concerned with construing meaning from experience as a guide to action (Mezirow, 1990). Such learning is self-directed, involves a willingness to take risks, and integrates what life teaches beyond formal education (Vaill, 1996).

Galbraith (1992) states, "lifelong education does not take place in a vacuum." A review of the framework for leading I suggested in the first chapter serves as an example of how this applies to leadership education. You will recall the phrase I used with two blanks to be filled in by you: LEADERSHIP FOR _____ WITH _____. We then proceeded to lay the groundwork for understanding leadership by looking at definitions and theories from the literature. You have been encouraged to consider what leading means to you. Next we considered the purpose of leadership which is, in simplest terms, to bring about changes. Your purpose and its context set the stage for you to reflect on your values and beliefs, the foundation of your personal philosophy of leadership. And, because leading doesn't happen in a vacuum either, we explored leadership as a relationship involving stakeholders and followers. Learning and leading both happen within a context.

What you have learned about purpose, context, and the people involved is the backdrop for deeper exploration of specific leadership concepts and acquisition of the relevant skills necessary to bring about desired change in your situation. Your learning will be a cyclic process much like that described by Kolb (1984). Kolb's learning cycle has the learner moving in circular fashion through four phases—observation and reflection, generalization and conceptualization, active experimentation, and concrete experience. As you observe and reflect on a concrete leadership experience, new ideas will occur to you from which you will make some generalizations. Then you try out these newly generated concepts in an active experimentation phase within your context for change. This, in turn, leads to another concrete experience on which you reflect—and the cycle continues. It may be encouraging to know that you do not need to have in-depth knowledge of every leadership concept and be able to employ every leadership skill before you are a leader. Learn what you need to know while you lead! The reality (and beauty) of shared leadership is that you do not need to know everything.

LEADERSHIP CONCEPTS AND SKILLS

Leadership concepts are generalized ideas or abstract notions concerning the process, relationships, and roles associated with leading. They represent real components of leaders' activities and are the means by which information is interpreted and organized. Cowan (1992) lists several examples of the range of attributions, behaviors, relationships, and so on, which comprise leadership concepts: authority, power, control, benevolence, consideration, conflict, politics, participation, delegation, decisions, courage, timing, inspiration, priorities, values, followers, groups, democracy, bureaucracy, and charisma. In many cases, once we uncover the concepts encompassed in our leadership situation, we will find out which skills we need to learn and practice to bring about intended changes.

Leadership skills refer to a set of proficiencies or abilities that evolve from understanding and practicing techniques that increase effectiveness. A wide range of skills may need to be developed by you, and those with whom you share leadership, to successfully bring about change. Perhaps the most fundamental skill leaders must have is the ability to communicate effectively. Communication skills include those required to speak in front of a group, listen reflectively, provide feedback, persuade, motivate, manage conflict, and debate, discuss, and engage a dialogue. Problem solving, goal setting, planning, and decision-making skills are essential and go hand in hand with resource management. Leaders must be able to build individual confidence and incorporate diverse perspectives while they nurture cooperation and teamwork. Effective leaders are able to identify and interpret values and culture. They can develop alternative scenarios and generate a vision for a preferred future. In addition, leaders must be able to think critically and creatively, using both right and left brain.

From my perspective, learning and applying appropriate skills to the leadership tasks brings us more to the middle of the leading-managing continuum referred to in Chapter 2 (see Figure 2.1). Thus, a discussion of leadership skill development is in a chapter near the end of *Leading from Within*, after you understand your leadership purpose, after you have a sense of who you are as a leader, and after you have explored relationships with stakeholders in your context for change. Just as you need to answer the question posed by Green (1992) earlier, "Leadership for what?" you must also ask yourself which skills need to be developed for your leadership purpose. To simply become proficient as a communicator, for example, does not mean that you suddenly become a leader. Instead, leaders learn while they lead, developing appropriate new skills needed within their context for change.

COMPETENCE AND COMPLEXITY

As you make plans to increase your effectiveness and your capacity to lead, you will want to pay attention to three different dimensions described by Apps (1994, p. 57): (1) the ability to reflect while acting and then make appropriate adjustments, (2) acquiring leadership competencies that apply to many leadership contexts, and (3) evolving a personal philosophy of leadership. We have dealt with the first and third dimensions in previous chapters. Let's look now at a framework that I have found useful in determining which skills and concepts need to be learned or enhanced to reach the level of competence desired.

Several years ago I met with a small group of community development experts in a retreat setting to discuss ways to encourage a national rural leadership focus with and for the Cooperative Extension System. Janet Ayers, a cohort from Purdue University, shared a handout in which she explained a leadership development continuum which she used for a program she introduced in Indiana. From her work, and from the retreat discussion, I developed a matrix for leadership education which I have used in many settings since then (see Figure 8.1).

I use this matrix first as a needs assessment tool, encouraging people to identify concepts and skills they wish to learn and to determine their current level of proficiency. In addition, I ask them to consider the setting within which they will employ the knowledge they seek. The skills they want to develop can be plotted in the matrix and success indicators can be determined for each level of competence. As leadership capacity increases, the matrix serves as a tool to track levels of competence and to plan for learning new skills.

As you look at the matrix, you will see that competency levels increase as you move from bottom to top of the matrix. The **awareness** level occurs when you recognize that knowing a skill will make a difference as you work to bring about intended changes. Your attention is drawn to the need or desire to know more about the underlying principles of a particular skill. The next level, **conceptualization**, is reached when you are able to

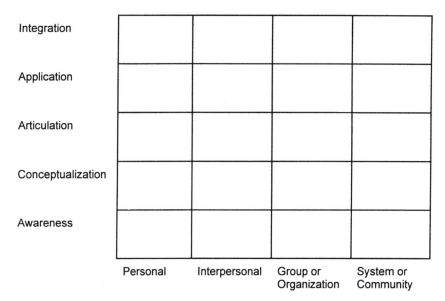

Figure 8.1 Leadership education matrix

understand the basic principles of the skill and to see how it might be important in your situation. Once you become familiar with the underlying concepts, you will be ready for the next level which is **articulation**. At this stage, you are able to explain the concept to another person. However, simply being able to describe a skill and its underlying concepts is not enough if you wish to put the skill to work within your context. When you begin to try out a new skill, you enter the **application** stage. At this level, you are able to apply what you have learned in a real life situation. This is the action phase of your leadership development effort. Ultimately, when you can apply the skills you are learning in a number of settings, transferring what worked in one context to a different situation, then you have reached the **integration** level. The new skill becomes almost second nature and you have confidence in your ability to use it as needed.

The skills you are learning will vary depending upon the complexity of the situation in which they will be applied. The baseline of the matrix moves from simple to more complex as you go from left to right. When you focus on **personal** skills, you will be learning for you own development as a leader. Clarifying values, beliefs, attitudes and assumptions as outlined in Chapter 5 falls in this area. When you are developing one-on-one relationships, **interpersonal** skills become more important. Listening and providing feedback, valuing others, and negotiating are examples of interpersonal skills. Much of what you do as a leader will involve a **group or organization**. You will need to develop the ability to manage conflict, create shared meaning, and build collaborative teams as part of this set of skills. The most complex situation in which you will lead is when you are involved in a **system or community** effort. In these instances, you might be working with several interrelated groups or with an organization with branches throughout the country. Very often, when the context for change is this complex, it becomes impossible to get everyone together in the same place to bring about intended changes. Thus, the communication skills needed will be much different than those that were useful in an interpersonal relationship. You will also want to learn to be adept at dealing with ambiguity, finding common ground, building coalitions, and strategic planning.

USING THE MATRIX: TWO EXAMPLES

The skills and concepts used as examples throughout this discussion are representative, but certainly not exhaustive. You will discover many more as you continue to learn and lead. At this point, let's use one skill as an example to demonstrate how the matrix might be used.

Goal setting is an important skill in any leadership context. In Mary's story at the beginning of Chapter 4, she became aware of a need for change and recognized that this would mean a new long-range goal for her life. She understood that goal-setting principles included visioning and prioritizing which would incorporate both critical analysis and creative thinking. However, she wanted to know more about how to set goals that were lofty enough to motivate her, but not unattainable to the extent that they seemed overwhelming. As she talked with family and friends about the process she was going through, she became more proficient at articulating just what she wanted to do—lead people to better health through massage therapy and wellness education. At this point, she began applying goal-setting skills by determining interim goals that would help her achieve her long-range purpose. She prioritized learning needs and financial obligations so that she could accomplish her goal. Now, she automatically sets her next goals as she continues to learn and practice her profession. In addition, she is quite adept at encouraging others to explore priorities and determine their personal wellness goals. Mary's goal-setting skills are now integrated into the work she does with clients on a daily basis.

Skipping over the next two columns, let's look at the right hand side of the matrix and consider developing competency in goal-setting processes within communities and systems. In this case, we can examine the story about the Partners' Project at the beginning of Chapter 6. It is immediately apparent that the skills appropriate for personal goal setting needed to be modified for use with the numbers of people involved. Additionally, a sense of the complexity is associated with trying to incorporate multiple perspectives embedded in the culture of various groups which may lead to conflicting priorities. Some of the underlying principles we needed to learn about included diversity, conflict management, collaboration, and coalition building. These concepts were discussed in community meetings and people began to articulate cultural differences as they searched for common ground. There was recognition that continued competition for resources would ultimately have a negative effect on all concerned. We looked for ways to apply what we were learning about collaboration as the Friends of the Santa Cruz evolved into a coalition with a set of long-term goals. Not everyone agreed on each issue, but the overarching goal to work together toward a safe, adequate water supply became integrated into decision-making processes. Collaborative goal setting has become a way of operating for the Friends of the Santa Cruz.

These two examples demonstrate how the Leadership Education Matrix might serve as the touchstone for the design of

continued learning for leaders. It is not intended to be the starting point for learning and leading. Rather, it is a reference point,
a developmental tool to be incorporated in your personal learning plan.

A PERSONAL PLAN FOR LEARNING
AND LEADING

Keeping in mind your purpose for leading and the changes
you intend to bring about, the following guidelines (adapted
from Apps, 1994) will aid in the development of your plan for
continuing to learn and lead:

1. Explore and describe fully the context within which you
   lead

2. Know who you are as a leader

3. Reflect on your values and beliefs

4. Identify and make plans to involve stakeholders

5. Develop your personal mission and vision statements

6. Determine long-range goals for yourself as a leader

7. Decide which concepts and skills you want to learn more
   about

8. For each concept and skill you want to learn, write down
   your objectives and progress indicators

9. Generate a list of approaches and resources that will help
   you attain your learning objectives

10. Continually reflect on your experiences as your plan evolves

As your learning plan evolves, consider a variety of educational
opportunities. Although reading is useful and helps us to form
new ideas, participation in workshops, seminars, and other experiential learning is invaluable. Through interaction and the
development of relationships with others who are actively en-

gaged in learning and leading, your perspective (and theirs) will be enhanced. You will be challenged to think outside yourself, and you will have cohorts with whom you can practice the concepts and skills you are learning. Perhaps your single most valuable learning tool, however, is your capacity to reflect and generate meaning from all that you do while learning and leading.

SUMMARY

Being a leader means being a learner. Your learning has been constant as you have made the phrase LEADERSHIP FOR _____ WITH _____ your own. This chapter has brought you to the point where you can now decide what skills and concepts you need to learn to effectively bring about the changes you intend. The Leadership Education Matrix is a useful tool for designing your own course of study for learning and leading and can be applied to any leadership context, now and in the future. In the final chapter of *Leading from Within*, we will deal with some aspects of leadership which, rather than skills and concepts to be learned, are personal choices that you make as a leader.

REFLECTION, APPLICATION, AND RESOURCES

Questions for Reflection and Journaling:

1. Think about leaders you know. In what ways are they life-long learners?

2. Think about lifelong learners you know. In what ways are they leaders?

Learning activities:

1. List fifteen or twenty leadership skills you think are important. Then, decide your level of expertise for each one using

the leadership education matrix as a guide. Also determine the level of complexity with which you are comfortable using these skills—personal, interpersonal, group, or community. You should be able to plot your current level of learning in this way.

2. Using your personal assessment from question one, set your learning goals for the skills you most want to develop. What are some success indicators that will help you to know when you've mastered each skill? Now you're ready to develop your personal learning plan! How will you acquire these skills?

3. Locate a copy of Cliff Hakim's book, *We Are All Self-Employed*. On page 141, you will find a tool for determining your level of commitment to continuous learning. Compare the items in the two columns and note the characteristics which describe you. For example, do you defend what you do and how you do it as the best or only way, or do you stay open to the possibility that you can learn new methods, improve your performance, and increase your productivity?

Suggested readings and resources:

1. Clark's article called "Transformational Learning" in S. B. Merriam's *An Update on Adult Learning Theory*, links understanding the nature of transformational learning with an exploration of philosophical assumptions about humans, knowledge, and society.

2. Larraine Matusak's book, *Finding Your Voice: Learning to Lead Anywhere You Want to Make a Difference*, includes a very helpful section (starting on page 154) on setting personal leadership development goals.

3. Hakim has a chapter called "Committing to Continuous Learning" in *We Are All Self-Employed*. You may find this useful as you reflect on your learning and leading.

4. Although I struggle with his use of the word training as it

refers to leadership education, Jay Conger's book, *Learning to Lead: The Art of Transforming Managers into Leaders*, has much to offer.

5. *Managers As Mentors: Building Partnerships for Learning* by C. R. Bell presents the other side of the story. If you want to know more about the role of mentor in leadership development, this is an excellent book.

6. Vaill's *Learning As a Way of Being* is strongly recommended. In particular, see Chapter 2, "Learning as a Way of Being: All Experience Is Learning."

CHAPTER 9

Being a Leader

Throughout *Leading from Within*, my intent has been to encourage you to be a leader, to do leadership. I expect you to be a leader because it is my conviction that we are all called to lead. I also believe that leadership is most often a shared activity as leaders serve while they lead and lead while they serve. Being a leader has to do with your spiritual aspect, who you are at your core; doing leadership is oriented toward your purpose, what you do to serve your reason for leading.

I have provided suggestions for what being a leader means within the context of each chapter. I've done the same for what doing leadership means. In the preceding chapter, the focus was almost entirely on what many people consider doing leadership, acquiring and applying the skills that you need for your personal development to be effective within your context for change. The final chapter of *Leading from Within* will elaborate on what being a leader means, the personal choices that are manifested whenever you lead. Leaders can learn how to gather and analyze information to make informed decisions. However, information doesn't make decisions, people do. Decision-making skills are necessary, but not sufficient. When leaders are asked to make choices which are expected to support the best interest of community, they recognize that some decisions are of the heart, choices to be made by tapping the inner spirit guiding us as we lead.

Some would say that what I refer to as choices are the qualities of an effective leader. For example, concern for people is a quality we look for in those who exercise decision-making skills in their efforts to bring about change in the communities where we live and work. It is one of many leader qualities enumerated in the literature. Apps (1994) mentions passion, perspective, balance, spiritually, courage, and tolerance for paradox, for example. Surveys done by Kouzes and Posner (1993) elicited twenty or more characteristics of effective leaders. The four most frequently mentioned were honesty, forward-looking, inspiring, and competent. A discussion concerning whether keen insight is the underlying leadership trait is found in Hughes, Ginnett and Curphy (1993). D'Antien (1993) would add intuition to the list. Covey (1991) describes three character traits: integrity, maturity, and an abundance mentality. Greenleaf's (1991) servant leaders are understanding, empathetic, intuitive, and aware. The United States Department of Education (1996) highlights passion, humor, empathy, strength of character, wisdom, common sense, and patience. These and many other aspects of personality said to be found in those who lead can be cited in the current literature.

PASSION, AUTHENTICITY, CREDIBILITY, AND ETHICS

There are four characteristics of effective leaders which I consider foundational. They are not traits which you are either born with or not. Neither are they attributes that you might acquire by learning more about them. I believe these essential leader characteristics are choices that we make. Exemplary leaders are passionate, authentic, credible, and ethical.

I am convinced that there is a leader within each of us that will, at some point, wrestle with these choices. As we look within where decisions of the heart are determined, it becomes apparent that there is also a choice that we can't *not* make first. Before we choose to be passionate, authentic, credible, and ethical, we must first decide to trust—to believe in ourselves. We must trust that our lives have meaning and that everyone else's life has its purpose as well. This is what Jaworski (1996) points out in his discussion of the fundamental shifts of mind which occur when we actively seek and serve the higher purpose which gives meaning to our life. Accepting ourselves and each other as legitimate human beings is part of what he calls the unfolding, imagining ourselves as part of our ultimate dream. Later, he talks about relatedness as a fundamental mode of existence, one that is grounded in a way of being rather than in doing, and claims that this is what has been missing in how we think about leadership. "We're always talking about what leaders *do*—about leadership style and function—but we put very little emphasis on the *being* aspect of leadership" (pp. 57–58). Choices concerning passion, authenticity, credibility, and ethics are those that shape a way of being, that help us know who we are when we are being leaders.

Passion

Purpose and passion go hand in hand. To be an effective leader, you must first care. When you care deeply, you have a passion that is more than simply the spark that gets you started, it is the fire inside that will sustain you. It is a commitment so compelling that your whole self—body, mind, and spirit—is engaged. Passion is energizing, enabling you to tap inner resources, strengths, and talents that you may have been unaware existed. On a cautionary note, you cannot be passionate about everything!

Go deep inside yourself to find the core of your concern and then follow where your heart calls. Believe that all you will need will be available to you. However, what you NEED may not always be what you WANT. By this I mean that sometimes you will experience failures along the way. "But if you meet setbacks and disappointments and challenges, and confront them with the same excitement and passion that you bring to your original ideas, you can transcend them to enjoy the fruits of your labors" (Kurtzig & Parker, 1991, p. 12).

Passion is not the same as a single-minded determination to get what you want or to create the changes you think should be made. Rather, passion for a higher purpose is characterized by an openness to possibilities and the innate belief that people want to work together to create the best future imaginable. Passion plus possibilities gives you courage! That is why creating a shared vision, one that is lofty and compelling, is so important. "A vision provides direction plus emotional appeal" (Apps, 1990, p. 21) and thus invokes passion. Choose what you will be passionate about and choose to be open to possibilities. Passion is a choice which has to do with integrity of the heart.

Authenticity

To be authentic is to be genuine. From my perspective, this means being who you are, all the time. If we pretend to be something we are not, we deceive twice. First, we deceive ourselves by trying to live out a belief that is not our own or engage in actions that we can't condone. The result of this self-deception over time is personal dysfunction. Avowals and actions that do not come from within eventually will conflict with the spirit at the core of each of us. I have seen people who continued to deny their own authenticity burn themselves out and experience mental and emotional collapse. To be authentic, however, frees us to be everything we were meant to be! We admit our shortcomings to ourselves, recognize our strengths, and live who we are.

The second deceit when we are not authentic is in our relationships. We cannot be fully integrated human beings if we try to be either less than or more than who we already are. Becoming chameleon-like just to please others is almost guaranteed to bring about disappointment and recrimination. When individuals feel the need to behave in a particular way while at work and not be the person they know themselves to be at home or with friends, something has to give. The opposite of integration is disintegration. The result is either an implosion or an explosion of the self.

Terry (1993) writes of the underlying notion of authenticity in leadership: "Authenticity entails action that is both *true* and *real* in *ourselves* and in the *world*. We are authentic when we discern, seek, and live into truth as persons in diverse communities and in the real world" (pp. 111–112). I believe that much of the disconnectedness we sometimes feel grows out of a need for authenticity. We long for genuine, trustworthy interac-

tion where we live and work, and we experience fulfillment
when our relationships with others are honest and grounded in
the truth of who we are. You can't force others to be authentic,
but authenticity is a choice for personal integrity that each of us
can make.

Credibility

If you are to have credibility, you must do what you say
you will do. Your reputation as a credible person develops as a
direct result of the trust others have in you to follow through,
acting on what you have committed yourself to do. Kouzes and
Posner (1987) claimed that "Leaders stand up for their beliefs.
. . . They show others by their own example that they live by the
values that they profess. . . . It is consistency between words and
actions that builds a leader's credibility" (p. 187). The authors
later wrote about three linked activities which strengthen leadership credibility—clarity, unity, and intensity. "By clarifying
meaning, unifying constituents, and intensifying actions, leaders demonstrate their own commitment to a consistent set of expectations. This process, repeatedly followed, earns leadership
credibility and sustains it over time" (Kouzes & Posner, 1993,
p. 48).

From the study cited in their book, Kouzes and Posner
(1993) have teased out common themes which represent credibility in practice. They cite six disciplines of credibility and go
on to describe each of them in an ensuing chapter. These disciplines are (1) discovering yourself, (2) appreciating constituents,
(3) affirming shared values, (4) developing capacity, (5) serving
a purpose, and (6) sustaining hope. Self-discovery encompasses
the development of a personal philosophy and credo statement—knowing what you stand for and where your limits are
regarding values and beliefs. Appreciating constituents means
recognizing the worth of others and being able to incorporate
multiple perspectives. Affirming shared values is one of the keys
to community building and is an ongoing process. Developing
capacity is the willingness to share leadership coupled with a
commitment to providing opportunity to learn and practice

good leadership. Serving a purpose means both acting as a servant leader and having a reason to lead, a higher cause that is not simply self-serving. Sustaining hope, it seems to me, takes a combination of inspiration, compassion, and recognition of the efforts of those who are encouraging positive change.

From my perspective, credibility begins with being authentic and is manifested in the actions you promise AND deliver. It is being accountable for what you say you will do. Whereas authenticity is grounded in personal integrity, credibility is the choice you make for interpersonal integrity.

Ethics

Ethical leaders have at the center of their belief system a high regard for human worth and dignity. They make decisions and take action in accord with these deeply held values and beliefs. Apps (1991, p. 113) offers the following as "touchstones for ethical decision-making":

- A fundamental concern for human beings
- Respect for justice and individual human rights
- Love for the earth
- Concern for quality above expediency
- Valuing a search for truth
- An appreciation of beauty

This list was developed within the context of teaching, but it is broadly applicable.

Making ethical decisions is not the same as taking an ethical stand on a social issue. In a leadership role, you are called upon to weave through multiple perspectives, presenting a variety of points of view. However, when asked, you have an ethical responsibility to yourself to clarify and claim your own beliefs with regard to social issues.

In his description of the servant-leader, Greenleaf (1991) says that servant leadership begins with a natural feeling that one wants to serve—one is servant first before consciously choosing to lead. He follows with this paragraph:

> The difference manifests itself in the care taken by the servant—first to make sure that other people's highest priority needs are being served. The best test, and difficult to administer, is: do those served grow as persons; do they, *while being served* [italics in the original], become healthier, wiser, freer, and more autonomous, more likely themselves to become servants? *And* [italics in the original], what is the effect on the least privileged in society; will [they] benefit, or, at least, will [they] not be further deprived? (p. 7)

From my vantage point, this exemplifies ethical leadership. "Leadership is ethical because of the relationship of ethics to authentic action" (Terry, 1993, p. 156). Service to others and a commitment to the greater good for more people is the essence of what it means to be ethical. Being ethical is a choice you make when passion, authenticity, and credibility are aligned with a belief system which is grounded in service to the global community. It is a matter of integrity with your soul.

Being a leader means recognizing passion, authenticity, credibility, and ethics as the cornerstones of effective leadership upon which we lay the foundation to bring about change. And these are personal choices, not simply what we come to know by studying about leaders and leadership. Bennis and Nanus (1985) capture the essence of what this means: "While we can elucidate as clearly as possible the principles we've been able to learn from our effective leaders, the process of internalizing them is a lifetime challenge" (p. 228). The need to do this inner work, to knowingly make these personal choices, is reiterated by Palmer (1996) when he says that a "leader is a person who must take special responsibility for what's going on inside him- or herself, inside his or her consciousness" (p. 35). Being a leader means knowing who you are at the deepest level.

SUMMARY

Leading from Within has taken you through an exploration of the meaning of leadership and your purpose for leading. You have probed the context within which you want to bring about change. You have begun to develop your personal philosophy of

leadership and written a credo statement. You briefly examined
the interdependent roles of leaders, followers, and stakeholders,
gaining a sense of the ways people come together to build community. You were introduced to a planning tool to select skills
and concepts for your continuing leadership development. And
finally, you pondered leadership qualities and your own choices
regarding passion, authenticity, credibility, and ethics. This is
where the book ends. The journey, however, continues. Being a
leader, doing leadership is the path you take when you care
enough to make a difference.

No one can teach you what your heart and soul expect of
you as a leader. That type of learning is a private matter. However, your decisions and actions as a leader will make your heart
and soul visible. When you lead, it is a reflection of who you are
inside. Your mind can grasp and apply new skills, understand
new leadership concepts, incorporate multiple perspectives, and
integrate new learning as you lead. Your body can express your
emotions, from joy to anger, from compassion to sorrow, and it
will carry out the actions that your mind decides are appropriate
for the changes you intend to bring about. Your spirit listens to
your soul and is the reflection of your moral nature. The soul
determines your behavior as a leader. Being a leader and doing
leadership means synchronizing the soul with your purpose for
leading. Each time you fill in the blanks in the phrase LEAD-
ERSHIP FOR _____ WITH _____, ask if the
leader inside you is committed to the purpose and the people,
with heart and soul. The potential to be a lifelong learner and
a leader is within each of us. The choices are yours.

REFLECTION, APPLICATION, AND RESOURCES

Questions for reflection and journaling:

1. What have others told you about yourself as a leader? What
   do you tell yourself about what kind of leader you are? What
   do you really know about yourself as a leader?

2. What are you most passionate about as a leader?

3. To what extent do you believe you can be who you are all the time? Are there barriers to your authenticity at work, with friends, or at home?

4. Have you ever promised too much and then found you couldn't do what you said you would do? If so, how did you handle it?

5. Do you always tell the truth? Are there certain conditions under which you might feel it unethical to tell the truth?

Learning activities:

1. Imagine that someone has built a measuring device to determine the extent to which you are passionate about your purpose for leading. Draw a picture or diagram of what it might look like, or build one out of Tinker Toys. What sorts of things would it measure? How would it measure them?

2. Listen to the news carefully or read a news magazine that provides some depth of analysis to headline stories. Find someone to discuss some of the decisions that world leaders are making? What are the ethical considerations associated with these decisions? What would you do differently? Why?

Suggested readings and references:

1. Peters and Austin wrote *A Passion for Excellence: The Leadership Difference* with a focus on the corporate sector. Their book has much to offer in your exploration of passion.

2. In *Paradoxes of Learning: On Becoming an Individual in Society*, Jarvis discusses authenticity in depth throughout chapters three and four. For another view, see pages 95–104 in Peter Block's book, *The Empowered Manager*, in which he discusses what he calls "authentic tactics."

3. Kouzes and Posner's book, *Credibility*, is highly recommended!

4. *Value and Ethics in Organization and Human Systems Development*, by Gellerman, Frankel, and Ladenson has a sec-

tion on confronting values and ethics, another on how to develop a statement of ethics and values, and a third section which presents several cases for discussion and learning.

5. Not your typical leadership book, Bolman and Deal's *Leading with Soul* is delightful and insightful. Every potential leader should read it!

6. *Synchronicity: The Inner Path of Leadership* is the story of Joseph Jaworski's personal journey. He candidly discusses deep leadership issues, ethical concerns, and future challenges for leaders.

REFERENCES

Adams, R. (1975). *Watership down.* New York: Avon Books.

Anderson, W. T. (1990). *Reality isn't what it used to be.* San Francisco: HarperCollins.

Apps, J. W. (1973). *Toward a working philosophy of adult education.* New York: Publications in Continuing Education.

Apps, J. W. (1990, fall). Beliefs, values and vision making for continuing higher education. *Continuing higher education review, 54* (3), 124–136.

Apps, J. W. (1991). *Mastering the teaching of adults.* Malabar, FL: Krieger.

Apps, J. W. (1992). Next age leadership transformation. *NELD Update, 1* (2) 1–2.

Apps, J. W. (1994). *Leadership for the emerging age: Transforming practice in adult and continuing education.* San Francisco: Jossey-Bass.

Autry, J. (1991). *Love and profit: Finding the balance in life and work.* New York: Avon Books.

Baldwin, C. (1990). *Life's companion: Journal writing as a spiritual quest.* New York: Bantam Books.

Bass, B. M. (1990). *Bass & Stogdill's handbook of leadership: Theory, research, and managerial applications* (3rd ed.). New York: Free Press.

Bell, C. R. (1996). *Managers as mentors: Building partnerships for learning.* San Francisco: Berrett-Koehler.

Bennis, W. G. (1959). Leadership theory and administrative behavior: The problem of authority. *Administrative Science Quarterly, 4,* 259–301.

Bennis, W. G. (1989a). *On becoming a leader.* Reading, MA: Addison-Wesley.

Bennis, W. G. (1989b). *Why leaders can't lead.* San Francisco: Jossey-Bass.

Bennis, W. G., & Nanus, B. (1985). *Leaders: The strategies for taking charge*. New York: Harper & Row.

Block, P. (1987). *The empowered manager: Positive political skills at work*. San Francisco: Jossey-Bass.

Block, P. (1993). *Stewardship: Choosing service over self-interest*. San Francisco: Berrett-Koehler.

Bogue, E. G. (1994). *Leadership by design: Strengthening integrity in higher education*. San Francisco: Jossey-Bass.

Bolman, L. G., & Deal, T. E. (1995). *Leading with soul: An uncommon journey of spirit*. San Francisco: Jossey-Bass.

Borich, T. O., & Foley, M. E. (1990, May). *Tomorrow's leaders today: Redefining the rural community*. Paper presented at the National Rural Studies Committee, Third Annual Meeting, Oregon State University, Corvallis.

Bryson, J. M., & Crosby, B. C. (1992). *Leadership for the common good: Tackling public problems in a shared-power world*. San Francisco: Jossey-Bass.

Burns, J. M. (1978). *Leadership*. New York: Harper & Row.

Buzan, T. (1983). *Using both sides of your brain*. New York: E. P. Dutton.

Campbell, D. P. (1991). *Campbell leadership index manual*. Minneapolis: National Computer Systems.

Campbell, S. (1995). A sense of the whole: The essence of community. In K. Gozdz (Ed.), *Community building: Renewing spirit and learning in business* (pp. 189–196). San Francisco: New Leaders Press.

Capra, F. (1975). *The tao of physics*. New York: Bantam Books.

Chaleff, I. (1995). *The courageous follower: Standing up to and for our leaders*. San Francisco: Berrett-Koehler.

Clark, R. (1992). *Building coalitions*. Columbus, OH: The Ohio Center for Action on Coalition Development for Families and High Risk Youth.

Clark, M. C. (1993). Transformational learning. In S. B. Merriam (Ed.), *An update on adult learning theory* (pp. 47–56). San Francisco: Jossey-Bass.

Conger, J. A. (1992). *Learning to lead: The art of transforming managers into leaders*. San Francisco: Jossey-Bass.

Cornesky, R. A. (Ed.). (1992). *Using Deming to improve quality in colleges and universities*. Madison, WI: Magna Publications.

Covey, S. R. (1989). *The 7 habits of highly effective people*. New York: Simon & Schuster.

Covey, S. R. (1991). *Principle-centered leadership*. New York: Summit Books.

Cowan, D. (1992). Understanding leadership through art, history, and arts administration. *Journal of Management Education, 16* (3), 272–289.

D'Antien, M. (1993). Intuition in the midst of change: A key to success in business. In P. Barrentine (Ed.), *When the canary stops singing: Women's perspectives on transforming business* (pp. 209–221). San Francisco: Berrett-Koehler.

De Angelis, B. (1995). *Confidence: Finding it and living it*. Carson, CA: Hay House.

Drath, W. H., & Palus, C. J. (1994). *Making common sense: Leadership as meaning-making in a community of practice*. Greensboro: Center for Creative Leadership.

Earnest, G. W. (1994, Fall). Power is a relationship. *The Leadership Journey, 3* (4), 1–6.

Fairholm, G. W. (1991). *Values leadership: Toward a new philosophy of leadership*. New York: Praeger.

Fiedler, F. E. (1967). *A theory of leadership effectiveness*. New York: McGraw-Hill.

Flora, C. B., Flora, J. L., Spears, J. D., Swanson, L. E., Lapping, M. B., & Weinberg, M. L. (1992). *Rural communities: Legacy and change*. Boulder, CO: Westview.

Galbraith, M. W. (1992). Lifelong education and community. In M. W. Galbraith (Ed.), *Education in the rural American community* (pp. 3–19). Malabar, FL: Krieger.

Gardner, J. W. (1990). *On leadership*. New York: Free Press.

Gellerman, W., Frankel, M. S., & Ladenson, R. F. (1990). *Values and ethics in organization and human systems development: Responding to dilemmas in professional life*. San Francisco: Jossey-Bass.

Goldberg, N. (1986). *Writing down the bones: Freeing the writer within*. Boston: Shambhala.

Gozdz, K. (1995a). Building a core competence in community. *The Systems Thinker, 6* (2), 8–12.

Gozdz, K. (1995b). Creating learning organizations through core competence in community building. In K. Gozdz (Ed.), *Community building: Renewing spirit and learning in business* (pp. 57–67). San Francisco: New Leaders Press.

Gray, B. (1989). *Collaborating: Finding common ground for multiparty problems*. San Francisco: Jossey-Bass.

Green, M. F. (1992). Developing effective leaders: Can it be done? *Innovative Higher Education, 17* (1, Fall), 57–69.

Greenleaf, R. K. (1991). *The servant as leader.* Indianapolis, IN: The Robert K. Greenleaf Center.

Greenleaf, R. K. (1996). *On becoming a servant leader.* San Francisco: Jossey-Bass.

Hakim, C. (1994). *We are all self-employed: The new social contract for working in a changed world.* San Francisco: Berrett-Koehler.

Handy, C. (1989). *The age of unreason.* Boston: Harvard Business School Press.

Hateley, B., & Schmidt, W. H. (1995). *A peacock in the land of penguins: A tale of diversity and discovery.* San Francisco: Berrett-Koehler.

Harris, T. A. (1967). *I'm ok—you're ok: A practical guide to transactional analysis.* New York: Harper & Row.

Hemphill, J. K. (1949). *Situational factors in leadership.* Ohio State University: Bureau of Educational Research.

Hemphill, J. K., & Coons, A. E. (1957). Development of the leader behavior description questionnaire. In R. M. Stogdill & A. E. Coons (Eds.), *Leader behavior: Its description and measurement.* Columbus: Ohio State University Personnel Research Board.

Hollander, E. P., & Julian, J. W. (1969). Contemporary trends in the analysis of leadership processes. *Psychological Bulletin, 17,* 387–397.

Huber, N. S. (1996). Leadership in higher education: Engaging the department heads. In *Leadership in a Changing World: Proceedings of the Annual Conference* (pp. 43–51). Burlington, VT: Association of Leadership Educators.

Hughes, R. L., Ginnett, R. C., & Curphy, G. J. (1993). *Leadership: Enhancing the lessons of experience.* Boston: Irwin.

Hunt, J. G. (1991). *Leadership: A new synthesis.* Newbury Park, CA: Sage.

Janov, J. (1995). Creating meaning: The heart of learning communities. *Training and Development, 49* (5), 53–58.

Jarvis, P. (1992). *Paradoxes of learning: On becoming an individual in society.* San Francisco: Jossey-Bass.

Jaworski, J. (1996). *Synchronicity: The inner path of leadership.* San Francisco: Berrett-Koehler.

Katz, D. & Kahn, R. L. (1978). *The social psychology of organizations* (2nd Ed.). New York: Wiley.

Kelley, R. (1992). *The power of followership.* New York: Doubleday Currency.

Kline, P. & Saunders, B. (1993). *Ten steps to a learning organization.* Arlington, VA: Great Ocean Publishers.

Kolb, D. A. (1984). *Experiential learning.* Englewood Cliffs, NJ: Prentice Hall.

Kouzes, J. M., & Posner, B. Z. (1987). *The leadership challenge.* San Francisco: Jossey-Bass.

Kouzes, J. M., & Posner, B. Z. (1993). *Credibility.* San Francisco: Jossey-Bass.

Kriegel, R. J., & Palter, L. (1991). *If it ain't broke . . . break it! and other unconventional wisdom for a changing business world.* New York: Warner Books.

Kurtzig, S. L., & Parker, T. (1991). *CEO: Building $400 million company from the ground up.* Boston: Harvard Business School Press.

Manning, G., Curtis, K., & McMillen, S. (1996). *Building community: The human side of work.* Cincinnati, OH: South-Western Publishing.

Margulies, N. (1991). *Mapping inner space.* Tucson, AZ: Zephyr Press.

Matusak, L. R. (1997). *Finding your voice: Learning to lead anywhere you want to make a difference.* San Francisco: Jossey-Bass.

Maynard, H. B., Jr. & Mehrtens, S. E. (1993). *The fourth wave: Business in the 21st century.* San Francisco: Berrett-Koehler.

McCall, M. W., Jr. (1993). Developing leadership. In J. R. Galbraith, E. E. Lawler III, & Associates (Eds.), *Organizing for the future: The new logic for managing complex organizations* (pp. 256–284). San Francisco: Jossey-Bass.

Metzger, D. (1992). *Writing for your life: A guide and companion to the inner worlds.* New York: HarperCollins.

Mezirow, J. (1990). A transformation theory of adult learning. In *Proceedings of the 31st Annual Adult Education Research Conference* (pp. 141–146). Athens, GA: University of Georgia Press.

Miller, L. C., Rossing, B. E., & Steele, S. M. (1992). *Partnerships: Shared leadership among stakeholders.* Madison: University of Wisconsin-Madison.

Moore, A. B., & Brooks, R. (1996). *Transforming your community: Empowering for change.* Malabar, FL: Krieger.

Munson, E. L. (1921). *The management of men.* New York: Holt.

Myers, I. B. (1962). *The Myers-Briggs type indicator.* Palo Alto, CA: Consulting Psychologists Press.

Nanus, B. (1992). *Visionary leadership: Creating a compelling sense of direction for your organization.* San Francisco: Jossey-Bass.

Ostendorf, D., & Levitas, D. (1987). Education for empowerment and social action in rural America. *Mid-American Review of Sociology, 12* (1), 55–64.

Palmer, P. J. (1996). The leader within. *Noetic Sciences Review, 40,* 32–37, 45–47.

Parker, G. M. (1990). *Team players and team work: The new competitive business strategies.* San Francisco: Jossey-Bass.

Peters, T. J., & Austin, N. K. (1985). *A passion for excellence: The leadership difference.* New York: Random House.

Rost, J. C. (1991). *Leadership for the twenty-first century.* New York: Praeger.

Sallis, E. (1993). *Total quality management in education.* Philadelphia: Kogan Page.

Schmidt, W. H., & Finnigan, J. P. (1992). *The race without a finish line: America's quest for total quality management.* San Francisco: Jossey-Bass.

Schmidt, W. H., & Finnigan, J. P. (1993). *TQManager: A practical guide for managing in a total quality organization.* San Francisco: Jossey-Bass.

Scholtes, P. (1988). *The team handbook.* Madison, WI: Joiner Associates.

Senge, P. M. (1990). *The fifth discipline: The art and practice of the learning organization.* New York: Doubleday.

Senge, P. M., Roberts, C., Ross, R. B., Smith, B. J., & Kleiner, A. (Eds.). (1994). *The fifth discipline fieldbook: Strategies and tools for building a learning organization.* New York: Currency Doubleday.

Senge, P. M. (1995). Creating quality communities. In K. Gozdz (Ed.). *Community building: Renewing spirit and learning in business* (pp. 48–55). San Francisco: New Leaders Press.

Sergiovanni, T. J. (1990). Adding value to leadership gets extraordinary results. *Educational leadership, 47* (8), 23–27.

Silien, K., Lucas, N., & Wells, R. (1992). Understanding leadership: The role of gender, culture and assessment in building community on campus. *Campus activities programming, 25* (1), 28–37.

Snyder-Nepo, N. (1992). Leadership Paper #4—"Leadership Assessments: A Critique of Common Instruments." Available through the National Clearinghouse for Leadership Programs, University of Maryland, College Park.

Spears, L. (1995, October). Excerpts from opening remarks at The Soul of Leadership conference sponsored by the Greenleaf Center, Indianapolis, IN.

Stogdill, R. M. (1974). *Handbook of leadership: A survey of theory and research.* New York: Free Press.

Stogdill, R. M. (1950). Leadership, membership, and organization. *Psychological Bulletin, 47,* 1–14.

Tannenbaum, R., Weschler, I. R., & Massarik, F. (1961). *Leadership and organization.* New York: McGraw-Hill.

Tead, O. (1935). *The art of leadership.* New York: McGraw-Hill.

Terry, R. W. (1993). *Authentic leadership: Courage in action.* San Francisco: Jossey-Bass.

Tichy, N. M., & Devanna, M. A. (1986). *The transformational leader.* New York: Wiley.

United States Department of Education. (1996). Strong leadership essential to school reform. *OERI Bulletin,* (Fall/Winter), p. 4.

Vaill, P. B. (1989). *Managing as a performing art: New ideas for a world of chaotic change.* San Francisco: Jossey-Bass.

Vaill, P. B. (1996). *Learning as a way of being: Strategies for survival in a world of permanent white water.* San Francisco: Jossey-Bass.

Watkins, K. E., & Marsick, V. J. (1993). *Sculpting the learning organization: Lessons in the art and science of systemic change.* San Francisco: Jossey-Bass.

Weisbord, M. R. (1987). *Productive workplaces: Organizing and managing for dignity, meaning, and community.* San Francisco: Jossey-Bass.

Wheatley, M. (1992). *Leadership and the new science: Learning about organization from an orderly universe.* San Francisco: Berrett-Koehler.

Williams, R. H., & Stockmyer, J. (1987). *Unleashing the right side of the brain.* Lexington, Mass: Stephen Greene Press.

Yukl, G. A. (1981). *Leadership in organizations.* Englewood Cliffs, NJ: Prentice Hall.

Zlevor, G. (1994). Creating a new workplace: Making a commitment to community. *The Systems Thinker, 5* (7), 1–4.

INDEX

Name _____

Address _____

City _____

State _____ Zip _____

Krieger Publishing Company

P.O. Box 9542

Melbourne, FL 32902-9542

WE HOPE THAT YOU ENJOY THIS BOOK...

and that it will occupy a proud place in your library. We would like to keep you informed about other publications from **KRIEGER PUBLISHING**.

Please use this form to request future literature in up to four (4) categories.

Subject Categories

☐ Medical Sciences (C)	☐ Physical Sciences (S) (Geology, Geography,
☐ Psychology/Sociology (B)	Oceanography,Water/Soil
☐ Education/Communication (F)	Management, Astronomy,
☐ Anthropology/Philosophy (G)	Meteorology, Ecology,
☐ History/Religion (H)	Environmental Science)
☐ Engineering/Technology (J)	☐ Veterinary Medicine (V)
☐ Chemistry/Biochemistry (K)	☐ Adult Education (W)
☐ Mathematics/Statistics (N)	☐ Space Sciences/Physics (X)
☐ Business Sciences/Economics (P)	☐ Public History (Y)
☐ Biological Sciences (R)	☐ Herpetology (Z)
(Botany, Ecology, Zoology,	☐ Other _____
Biology, Nature)	

Name _____

Mailing Address _____

City _____

State _____ Zip _____ +4 _____

Country _____ Postal Code _____

(200M) 4/96 SHORT